BLOOM
& SHINE!

DAILY INSPIRATION TO HELP YOU BLOOM
AND SHINE THROUGHOUT THE YEAR

COMPILED BY
REBECCA HALL GRUYTER
#1 INTERNATIONAL BEST SELLING AUTHOR

RHG | MEDIA PRODUCTIONS™

Bloom & Shine!
Daily Inspiration to Help You Bloom and Shine Throughout the Year!

Copyright © 2020 by Rebecca Hall Gruyter

RHG Media Productions

25495 Southwick Drive #103

Hayward, CA 94544.

ISBN 978-1-7328885-6-2 (paperback)

Visit us on line at www.YourPurposeDrivenPractice.com

Printed in the United States of America.

ACKNOWLEDGMENTS

I want to thank all those experts who have come together with the common heartbeat of pouring into others on a daily basis. Thank you for entrusting us with your heart, wisdom, and inspiration.

Thank you to my husband, who helps uplift me to *Bloom & Shine*. You truly are the wind beneath my wings.

Thank you to my grandmothers, who always saw the best in me and taught me to stop, pause, and listen on a daily basis and so mindfully and purposefully choose what I echo out into the world.

Thank you to my parents for uplifting me, holding space, grounding me, and helping me step forward and shine. Thank you for showing me what it is like to be loved.

I thank God for this life and His amazing ability to turn challenges into blessings and gifts. With His strength, love, and support, we are able to rise up, no matter what, and share and shine out into the world.

Thank you to our readers who have leaned in and added this positive book to their libraries. May it uplift and encourage you to celebrate the gift that you are and be willing to share and shine out the gift of you to the world as you bloom and shine each and every day of the year.

TABLE OF CONTENTS

INTRODUCTION
BLOOM AND SHINE!
BY: REBECCA HALL GRUYTER, BOOK COMPILER

Thank you for leaning into *Bloom and Shine.* I'm honored and excited to bring this powerful book to you, featuring fourteen experts that are committed to helping you **shine** powerfully in your life! Our vision is that this amazing collection of 365 inspirations will walk beside you and support you each and every day of the year, year after year. Many of us have been powerfully served by daily inspiration books, and now we are honored to have the opportunity to walk beside you and support you on a daily basis.

As an empowerment leader, I know a lot about being disempowered and how to overcome that in order to step into your passion, power, and gifts so that you **shine**! I celebrate you saying "yes" to this book and to yourself! It is a courageous act to say "yes" to you and to be willing to let others walk beside you to support and cheer you on in life.

Life is not a solo journey, and the more we can walk beside each other and cheer each other on, the more rich and powerful our journey becomes. I believe the transformation and living a life on purpose takes place in the mindful choices we make on a day to day basis. And those choices add up to our week, our month, and our life. This daily inspiration book is designed to support you in stopping, pausing, and reflecting each day, pouring into you encouragement, truth, motivation, and support into you daily.

In sharing their inspirations, our authors will equip and empower you to discover your value, align to your purpose, step forward, and choose to **shine**! I believe this book is a living and interactive book that will speak wisdom, encouragement, and power into your life. Your heart will be touched, and you will be motivated and to take action to step forward powerfully in your life. I want to invite you to pause, take a deep breath, and be ready to receive these powerful messages so they can ignite a fire in you, inspire courage in you, and focus your purpose on your life to encourage you to take action now and **shine**!

We each need others to encourage us, to speak wisdom and truth into us, to love us and cheer us on, and to help us stand up again when we fall. This book will walk beside you to help you run and not grow weary, to complete all that you are called to complete, and to live on purpose and with great purpose.

In creating this book, I asked each heart-centered and powerful co-author to share a daily inspiration to support you, one day and one choice at a time. As they share from their respective journeys with you, they share what they have learned. They share their wisdom and what they wish someone had encouraged them with or whispered in their ear, especially in those dark and challenging times. They are committed to pouring into you and equipping and empowering you in your life. Throughout the inspirations, you will feel a consistent and transparent heartbeat to support you in very real ways as the authors often share what they wish they would have known. We want to make your path and journey easier for you step forward and **shine**! As the book compiler, I'm so proud of what each co-author has shared in their chapters and am honored to have each of them leaning in to support you. I am equally honored that you have said "yes" to our book and are entrusting us to support you on your journey.

Now, it's your turn. Are you going to lean in and learn from the wisdom within this book? Will you let us walk beside you on your journey of life? We want to lift you up, support you, encourage you, and empower you. It is your choice. We want to equip and empower you to take action, move forward, and share your gifts with the world. You can choose to open the pages and let them pour into you, or you can put this book on a shelf. My heart and prayer are that you will say "yes" to you and lean into the powerful messages of hope that are waiting to pour into you, your heart, and your life.

You have unique gifts, talents, abilities, stories, journeys, and perspectives that you alone can bring forward. Those in your life need you, your message, your wisdom, your perspective, gifts, talents, and heart. When we shrink back or hide, the world becomes less vibrant, and we all miss out. Be willing to share the gift of you with those around you and with the world! Be willing to be seen on the same level you are willing/wanting to serve.

Here is how to get the most out of this powerful book. It is divided into three sections, each one designed to meet you exactly where you are and to support you each and every day of the year. **In the first section,** you will find the daily inspiration in order of the calendar year, each month and day of the year. **In the second section,** you will find a subject section that you can look up a particular area or subject in which you want support, and it will list the inspirations that can support you in that particular area. **In the third section,** you will find all our beautiful authors' pictures, biographies, and contact information. I know that they would love to hear from you and have you follow and connect with them. I encourage you to "friend" and follow those authors with whom you feel a powerful resonance and connection so that they can continue to pour into and support you on your journey in life.

Now the next step is yours. Drink in the stories and messages that are within these pages to serve, support, and inspire you. Take the time to pause, read, and reflect. Listen to the powerful messages of hope that are waiting for you within the pages of this book. It's not an accident that you purchased this book and are opening it to read right now today. I invite you to lean in and truly receive the messages and wisdom that will speak to your heart and soul that you will find in these transformational and dynamic pages. Enjoy this rich collection of wisdom, love, and encouragement.

—Rebecca Hall Gruyter, Book Compiler

Founder/Owner of Your Purpose Driven Practice and CEO of RHG Media Productions

Rebecca Hall Gruyter is a global influencer, #1 international best-selling and award-winning author and compiler, in-demand publisher, Empowering radio show host (reaching over 1 million listeners on eight networks), podcast host, and an Empowerment leader that wants to help you reach more people. She has built multiple platforms to help experts reach more people. These platforms include: radio, TV, books, magazines, the Speaker Talent Search, and live events, creating a powerful promotional reach of over 10 million!

Rebecca is the CEO of RHG Media Productions (which includes the RHG TV network with over thirty weekly programs and a publishing arm that has helped over 250 authors become best-sellers). She is the owner of Your Purpose Driven Practice and the Creator of the Speaker Talent Search.

RHG Media productions is an in-demand publisher that specializes in launching books as best-sellers while creating great visibility both for the author and book. She helps the author be powerfully positioned and the star of their best-selling campaign to reach as many people as possible around the world.

Rebecca has personally contributed to over thirty published books, multiple magazines and has been quoted in Major Media, *The Huffington Post*, ABC, CBS, NBC, Fox, and Thrive Global. She has been recognized as one of the top-ten working women in America by AWWIN, Inc., and now helps experts get quoted in major media, too.

Today, she wants you to have impact! Be seen, heard, and *shine!*

Rebecca@YourPurposeDrivenPractice.com

www.facebook.com/rhallgruyter (Facebook)

www.YourPurposeDrivenPractice.com (Main website)

www.RHGTVNetwork.com (TV network)

www.SpeakerTalentSearch.com (Free opportunity for speakers to get on more stages)

www.EmpoweringWomenTransformingLives.com (Weekly radio show)

www.AuthorsJourneyPodcast.com (Weekly podcast for authors)

www.MeetWithRebecca.com (Calendar link to schedule a time to talk with Rebecca)

January

1.

There's Plenty of Room for You to Shine!

There's room for everybody to shine. Life is not a competition.

There is enough space for everyone to bloom into the amazing individual that they uniquely are. Just look up into the night sky, the expansive universe. One star doesn't take away from the others; it just *is* and knows itself and shines like it's the only beautiful star out there. And it knows that it is part of something even more expansive and beautiful.

Just look at your garden. One bloom doesn't diminish the other—in fact, its brilliant red looks even more spectacular next to the bright yellow daisy next to it. Both shine even brighter!

People sometimes say to me, "But what do I have to say that hasn't already been said?" Or, "If I highlight this person, then everyone will go to them instead of me!"

I tell them, "There is nobody who says or does it exactly as you do. The world needs to hear *you*, and there is room for you and everyone else in a world of abundance."

The brighter you *shine*, the more that is seen, and the more good you can do in this world—as the unique gift that you are!

—**Daily inspiration by Rebecca Hall Gruyter, Influencer and Empowerment Leader**

2.

Potential

"It takes courage to not only accept our limitations but embrace our potential."

—ERWIN RAPHAEL MCMANUS

January is a time when our thoughts often turn to how we are making a contribution to the world. Or how we are disappointed in past performance and look for ways to have a positive outcome going forward.

Congratulations! Now is a perfect time to rewrite your story to create the life you are designed to lead. We all can decide to do one thing today to start the journey to learn a new skill or explore a new way of thinking.

The best way to rewrite your story is to write about what makes your heart soar. Then choose one thing you can do today to make your dream a reality. Perhaps you make a list of what it would take to accomplish this thing. Or make a single phone call to start researching this topic.

When I decided to embrace my potential, I learned, for me, all roads lead to writing in some shape or form. No matter where I am, or what I am doing (at a business networking event, or standing in line at the grocery store), I am compelled to encourage everyone to recognize that their voice matters and the world is missing out when they choose to hide it. Be willing to share your hard-won wisdom. How will you embrace your potential today?

—Daily inspiration by Mary E. Knippel, Writer Unleashed

3.

Thought for the Day

"Two roads diverged in a wood, and I – I took the one less traveled by, And that has made all the difference.

—ROBERT FROST

4.

Step Forward into Growth

"In any given moment, we have two options: to step forward into growth or step back into safety."

—ABRAHAM MASLOW

Let's celebrate the new year with a new, even better version of *you!* The new year gives us the opportunity to step forward into growth rather than step back into the status quo.

Take a moment right now to think of one of the values or characteristics that you would like to have more of in the future. Perhaps it is acting more courageous, adventurous, creative, playful, or grateful—the list is unlimited.

Now, choose one quality and practice *being it* for the week or month, or the whole year if you like. For example, let's take "playful." How can you be less serious in various scenarios? Maybe you can remind yourself that it's okay to laugh at yourself or to act silly when quirky thoughts enter your mind. What does the version of you who is playful value in life? What does playfulness look like to you?

Committing to the choice automatically tunes you in to your awareness on a deeper level. You will expand into greater possibilities and choices for yourself as the new version of you. This will take practice to consistently show up for yourself as the new *you.*

Every choice creates awareness. Even if choices don't turn out the way you'd like, *you are not wrong.* You've taken a step forward into more awareness about what that choice created, and what you'd like *not* to choose next time.

—Daily inspiration by Dr. Kimberly Schehrer, Teen Breakthrough Expert

5.

Thought for the Day

"You become what you believe."

—OPRAH WINFREY

6.

Your Message Is Needed!

When an opportunity comes to you to show up in a bigger way, it often means that you are being called to step out in ways you hadn't thought of before.

For many of the authors we help publish, it's their first time writing for the public. Typically, they have reached out to us from a deep soul place: "I'm being called to bring my mission forward. I want to reach the people I'm supposed to reach."

We work with them to bring that mission out into the world. What often happens when we start out is that the person doesn't even realize the power of what they are about to bring forward. They have fears about whether their message is worth hearing or their mission worth following. They don't realize how wonderful they are, but we do!

One of my greatest joys is when they launch their book out into the world, and it becomes a national or international best-seller. Not so much to accumulate awards, but because **they get to acknowledge and affirm the influence they are having in the world.** They get to see what others see, and when the world receives it so powerfully (whether it's a book, a presentation, a TV/radio show, etc.), this, in turn, is transformational for others. It's part of the journey that we take together of shifting and expanding how we show up in the world. How are you holding space for yourself and others to shine?

—Daily inspiration by Rebecca Hall Gruyter, Influencer and Empowerment Leader

7.

Thought for the Day

*"Let your Spirit lead you and your
light will shine ever bright."*

—LESLIE C. DOBSON, YOU WERE MADE TO SHINE

8.

New Beginnings

"Celebrate endings, for they precede new beginnings."
—JONATHAN LOCKWOOD HUIE

Take a deep breath. Close your eyes and think about the new year. New beginnings.

Breathe in and think about everything good in your life. Breathe out anything negative from last year. You cannot change the past, so why dwell on that? Learn from it and move on.

Remember, each day affords you the ability for a new beginning, not just the new year.

It is not always easy, but it is always important to focus on the good in your life. Be grateful for what you have and live one day at a time. Remember to breathe.

—Daily inspiration by Dr. Sarah Breen

9.

Grounded in Your Truth as You Fly

*"Flying starts from the ground. The more
grounded you are, the higher you fly."*

—J.R. RIM

I believe it's important in all things that we do to stay grounded in our truth, our *why*. This is the key to living on purpose, blooming, shining, and soaring. We need to take the time to truly discover our *why*—our motivation and purpose. Once we gain clarity on our purpose, we are then able to know more easily what to say *yes* to and what to say *no* to.

We say *yes* to the things that matter most to us and to the things that will help us move forward. And then, we can confidently say *no* to the things that we know will move us further away from our purpose.

This keeps us grounded in our roots and in our truth and helps us *bloom*, to move forward into doing things that keep us more fully being all that we are called and created to be and to become. Our purpose will motivate us to take action even when we hit challenges. We now begin to *shine* in alignment without truth and spreading our light outward into the world. Then, the only way to go is up, to *soar*!

—Daily inspiration by Rebecca Hall Gruyter, Influencer and Empowerment Leader

10.

An Epic Invitation to Bloom and Shine

Happy New Year, dear reader! Welcome to the first month of your best year yet! I'm excited to travel together into "the great unknown" with you over these next twelve months! In fact, I've been looking forward to asking you a question: *what's your favorite way to start the new year* **strong**? One of my own special traditions is playing a song dating back to my student years at Boston College called "The Summons" by John L. Bell and Graham Maule. As you kick off the new year, I invite you to take a moment to reflect on a brief excerpt from this beautiful tune:

Will you love the "you" you hide if I but call your name?

Will you quell the fear inside and never be the same?

Will you use the faith you've found to reshape the world around?

through my sight and touch and sound in you and you in me?

There are people in your life *waiting* for you to unfold your beautiful potential and answer your call to lead and serve. In what area(s) of your life is this epic invitation personally summoning you to dare greatly, love deeply, bloom and *shine*? What's one mini (or giant) step you can take to make it happen in the year ahead? What accountability system will you rely on this year to stay encouraged and keep moving forward? (To listen to the complete song, visit:

https://www.youtube.com/watch?v=Y7Y5RWel6eg).

—Daily inspiration by Marlene Elizabeth, author of Moneywings™

11.

Thought for the Day

"Act as if what you do makes a difference. It does."

—WILLIAM JAMES

12.

Take the Stage!

Many powerful experts with valuable information, unfortunately, have difficulty finding and getting on stages (virtual as well as live) in front of the people who would most benefit from their knowledge and gifts.

Here are three keys to success that I've learned along the way:

Know there are stages available to you. Community leaders with speaking opportunities want great speakers for their audiences as badly as you want the chance to speak.

Know what stages are right for you. Take some time to identify and focus on the opportunities that are best for you, for example, your ideal audience, the size of the audience (especially if you're new to speaking), and if the host's concept of the experience is aligned with yours.

Connect from a place of service. Make sure to cultivate the spirit of service within yourself first before connecting with an opportunity—try seeing the world through the eyes of the person with whom you're trying to connect: what are they looking for? What are they most excited about? What solutions are they seeking for their people?

Know that the world needs the unique and wonderful gifts you bring. So, take the stage and *shine!*

—*Daily inspiration by Rebecca Hall Gruyter, Influencer and Empowerment Leader*

13.

Thought for the Day

"If you obey all the rules, you miss all the fun."

—KATHARINE HEPBURN

14.

Life Is for Us

"Life happens for us, not to us."

—TONY ROBBINS

This quote has been attributed to many over the years; however, perhaps Tony Robbins earns the original credit. The point is to look at what life does *for* us, to help us sharpen our skills, to prepare us for life's lessons, perhaps even to facilitate our gratitude. Yes, even in the tough times. I know sometimes a positive mental attitude is not easy, but it is simple. Attitude is a choice. Perspective is a choice. Take a moment to reflect on what is the highest good for everyone and choose wisely. Sometimes we need to take a step back and see life from a different angle. What could be the most challenging *at that moment* might just turn out to be one of life's most beautiful joys and our greatest triumphs. How is life working for you today?

—Daily inspiration by Dr. Cheryl Lentz, The Academic Entrepreneur

15.

Thought for the Day

"If God is your partner, make your plans BIG!"

—D.L. MOODY

16.

Persistence

Persistence Makes Good Things Happen

It is easy to give up after attempting something that fails. No one succeeds, especially consistently over time, by simply doing the right thing successfully every time they attempt something. I learned that if I attempt something and it doesn't immediately succeed or win, even if it is an overwhelming failure, that doesn't mean it can't succeed. I may have attempted it with the wrong audience or in the wrong location, or my timing was off. While one potential customer might have no interest in a product, plenty of others may love it. I have to give them a chance to discover it.

There is one, and only one, guaranteed way to fail: stop trying. You can't succeed when you stop trying. You need to find the right situation. This could include things like location, customers, and product or service in the right combination. Sometimes even those who reject you will change their minds later. Someone may not buy your book only because they have four others sitting on their desk at home. Someone may not buy your delicious ice cream cone only because they just started a diet. If they encounter your book or your ice cream cone at another time, they may buy and become your biggest fan and even a repeat customer.

—*Daily inspiration by Patrick P. Long, International Best-Selling Author*

17.

Thought for the Day

"We accept the love we think we deserve."

—STEPHEN CHBOSKY,
THE PERKS OF BEING A WALLFLOWER

18.

Embrace and Nurture the Potential of Your Uniqueness

No one came to this earth emptyhanded; no one is insignificant not to have a purpose, and no one is too poor to give, including you. **Every new beginning represents a promise, a fresh start full of possibilities for growth toward excellence, or something exceptional.** A blank canvas can bear the most beautiful artwork, the soil the most delicious fruits, a garden the most beautiful flowers, or an instrument a potential source for harmonious and beautiful melodies; you, too, have the potential to become an inspiration for many.

A January breeze with its fresh start is a reminder that you, too, have a unique gift called talent. You are a gift to this world, a seed of hope where rests latent a promise of beauty and a potential source of inspiration for generations. Like Gandhi, Martin Luther King, Jr., Mandela, and many who continue to inspire after their passing, you can build a beautiful legacy to survive you. Ride this refreshing wave of hope and new beginning to set in motion the Laws of Creation that will unleash your potential beyond your imagination. Like anything else that must yield something exceptional, your efforts and commitment are needed, and you must be patient with yourself. This is not a race but a journey. The difference between the race and a journey is that, in a race, crossing the finish line is only one goal, while a journey offers an infinite amount of possibilities and experiences to enjoy along the way to the destination.

—*Daily inspiration by Fabien W. Edjou, Author & Life Coach*

19.

Thought for the Day

"Life shrinks or expands in proportion to one's courage."

—ANAIS NIN

20.

New Beginnings

"I want to get you excited about who you are, what you are, what you have, and what can still be for you. I want to inspire you to see that you can go far beyond where you are right now."

—VIRGINIA SATIR

No matter where you are in your life, no matter if everything has fallen apart, every single moment, you have an opportunity to begin again. This moment you are experiencing is the result of everything you've created up until this moment. And right now, you can choose a new path. You can choose a new start. This is your day! Look back on last year as a freshly completed book. Ponder and separate out your experiences by taking three sheets of paper and at the top write: EMBRACE: What you liked; RELEASE: What you want to let go of; and DESIRE: What you want to create. Gather a large bowl, some matches, and go outside to a quiet place with your lists. Take the list of what you want to *release* and light it on fire over the bowl, saying, "I release myself from any ties to these experiences." When you can no longer hold the paper, drop it into the bowl. Now imagine cleansing white light filling the space in your being where the unwanted experiences were. Now read the EMBRACE and DESIRE lists out loud, feeling, and being fully engaged in the experience. These seeds will grow into vibrant blossoms when nurtured.

—*Daily inspiration by Kimi Avary, MA, Relationship Navigation Specialist*

21.

New Year Intentions

A new year. I always feel a lot of pressure this time of year. The whole "resolutions" thing always feels a little daunting to me. What if my resolve isn't strong enough? What if my lofty goals end up being broken promises by the end of January?

In the spirit of resting more and striving less, can I suggest taking some time this week to simply reflect? Take some to think about your life – about who you are now and who you want to become. Think through your various roles and responsibilities. Consider the things in your life that make you feel the most alive. Examine your inner life and evaluate the ways that you're spending your resources (time, money, and gifting). Reflect, brainstorm, evaluate, and dream.

It doesn't need to be fancy or formal. There's no right or wrong way to proceed. Just take the time to do it. Why?

(1) It will give you a chance to celebrate the beautiful! As you reflect on the last year, you'll be reminded of sweet memories and character milestones.

(2) It will help you be more intentional in the coming year. Perhaps there are ways you'll live differently or relationships you'll pursue anew, or changes you'll make in the way you organize your life.

And let's face it, we all know that nothing worth having/doing just comes naturally. You won't become a better spouse or parent, or friend by accident. It will take intentional effort. Effort that is borne out of this evaluation of your current reality. Be willing to reflect, dream, and plan your intentional effort.

—*Daily inspiration by Shannon McKee, Author, Mentor, and Life Coach*

22.

Thought for the Day

"It's not enough to have lived. We should be determined to live for something."

—WINSTON S. CHURCHILL

23.

Thought for the Day

"To shine your brightest light is to be who you truly are."

—ROY T. BENNETT

24.

Hibernation and Rebirth

A new year brings with it an indignant and unrelenting hope that the mistakes of yesteryear can be eased and then erased. Crisply chilled air fills our lungs and illuminates in steam clouds beneath snow-covered streetlights as we scrape the ice from our automobiles—a reminder that we can have warmth, but we must persevere through the trenches of snowbanks and challenges.

Clawing out of our mistakes, our longings, and our shortcomings, we now begin a hibernation and a rebirth simultaneously.

We focus on the renewal of our legacies. We focus on the triumphs yet to come. We bid our time until warmth re-emerges. May you celebrate the new year and all that is to come.

In January, I am inspired by the many hard lessons I have learned from, as I reflect on all of the ways I plan to build a better me for the year of evolution for which I cross my fingers. May you start the new year with purpose, looking for ways to bring forward the gift of you.

—*Daily inspiration by Leigh Bursey, Musician, Speaker, and Municipal Councillor*

25.

Your Word

Most years, I begin with a distinct word that creates my intention for the year. This year, 2020, my word is *persevere*. I will persevere through all my challenges. This is my strength and says no matter what I'm going through to keep moving forward.

Some of my other words were *imagine, health, release, accomplished,* and *success*.

How I decide which word is best for each year is by asking my angels. I trust their guidance because they have guided my journey and support me along the way. **These words have significance and represent your ultimate dreams.**

Another way I begin my year is by making vision boards and creation journals. If you never heard of these, it's a simple way to layout your goals. Using pictures and phrases, you will lay them out on your choice of poster/paper. Once you glue them all on, place your "board" in a place you will always see it. You can put your word of the year on top for added intentions.

What is your word of the year? Maybe meditate on it, analyze where you are in terms of your present life and where you would like to go.

—**Daily inspiration by Catherine M. Laub, Podcast Host**

26.

Thought for the Day

"You miss 100% of the shots you don't take."

—WAYNE GRETZKY

27.

Positive Tomorrows

We glance back at yesterday, where life was not made from rose petals with a sweet fragrance. Sometimes there were thorns in your life, such as a loved one that hurt you, relationships that caused you to cry, a career that you never were able to achieve, and children that caused you to be despondent.

Clifford Naas, a professor at Stanford University, did a study showing that people will listen and more thoroughly process negative emotions and experiences than positive ones. He stated that "the human mind will tend to remember more unpleasant events and will use more strong words to describe negative times than using words to describe happy moments."

It's not a time to live in the negative moments of the past and give up. No, not you! **It's time to rise and know you can begin again. It's time to use your choice. Choose to be positive.** John Marks Templeton quotes, "We always have a choice. We can become bitter, or we can choose to be bigger and better people. When we learn to recognize that every experience can bring a blessing of some kind, our upset is softened."

It's time to release that negative experience of stress and pain and find the blessing in it. **Use what you have; don't hide behind your past. Choose to stand tall and be the person that you are, hold your head up, and know you are somebody special!**

—*Daily inspiration by Toni Stone Bruce, Precious Stones 4 Life, LLC*

28.

Trust the Process

We are put on this earth with a purpose—something only we are meant to do.

When aligned with your purpose or calling, trust the process. Things will come, and you will find your way. How can you lean in and trust the process more?

—Daily inspiration by Maureen Ryan Blake, Founder and Principal of The Power of the Tribe

29.

Thought for the Day

*"One is loved because one is loved.
No reason is needed for loving."*

—PAULO COELHO, THE ALCHEMIST

30.

Success

I spent many years (too many) trying to follow someone else's definition of success because I didn't have my own. I don't anymore because I've explored and **discovered my own definition of success.**

If we don't have clarity on our definition of success (personal, business, and financial), we frequently end up following someone else's by default because we don't have our own. I find this to be a big mistake that leads to chasing down dreams that are not your own. And this almost always leads to disillusionment, discouragement, and burnout. Do you know your definition of success?

Your definition of success is as personalized as your wardrobe, furniture, and what's in your refrigerator! It's easy to think about how the "grass is greener on the other side" for that person whose dream we think we want to follow. But we're only looking at part of the picture (the one we want to believe), and we don't really know what's going on behind the scenes for these people. So, it becomes chasing rainbows.

Take some time to do this simple yet powerful exercise. Ask yourself: **How do I define success in my life, my business [or another aspect in your life that's important to you]?** Have that deep conversation about where you are now, where you want to go, and how you want to get there. Get some clarity on what it would look like to live a life and have a business that is meaningful to you!

—Daily inspiration by Rebecca Hall Gruyter, Influencer and Empowerment Leader

31.

Thought for the Day

"Seventy percent of success in life is showing up."

—WOODY ALLEN

February

1.

Learn to Dance with Fear

Have you ever noticed that the more you try to avoid fear, the more it seems to grow and take you over? I have learned to "dance" with fear—move with it and through it, not avoid or run from it.

Think of fear as an indicator of stepping out of your familiar comfort zone into a new place. If you want to go where you haven't been before and serve in new ways, then you're choosing to move out of your comfort zone.

It is your choice to move forward or stay where you are.

Be willing to be a little uncomfortable (for a while) to build what you're called to build and be what you're called to be. What helps me through my fear is remembering my "why" and that my choice is voluntary. I just take one step at a time, pulled forward by my purpose of bringing truth, empowerment, choice, and value into someone's life.

Fear is temporary; the rewards of the dance last a lifetime!

—*Daily inspiration by Rebecca Hall Gruyter, Influencer and Empowerment leader*

2.

Thought for the Day

"The earth is gentle. And the earth allows the flowers to bloom. We need to be gentle. And the flowers will bloom in our life."

—AVIJEET DAS

3.

Love—Agape

"It's not the people in our lives who make our lives, but loving them does."

—ANONYMOUS, HALLMARK CHANNEL

Love is your birthright. Love is a universal force, and by its nature, it is everywhere. Small hurts from grief and loss build up over time, and as it does, our natural response is to protect ourselves. Our natural tendency is to build a shield around our hearts. Over time this shield becomes thicker until it becomes an impenetrable barrier keeping perceived danger out but also keeping your essence inside.

And what of your heart? Isolated and alone, it begins to wither. It may even feel like the capacity to love is dead, but in truth, it cannot die. **You are a being of love. It is the essence of who you are.** Are you feeling the love today? If not, pause and remember a moment where you experienced love, no matter how small. Feel it. Fan the flames. Allow it to grow. You can do this! Let it fill up your heart and spread to your entire body. Feel it vibrate in every cell of your body. What color is it? Does it have a sound? A smell? What does it taste like? Imagine love pouring out of you in waves and touching everyone and everything around you. See it spreading to everyone near you. Envision it enveloping your home, your town, your country, and the world. **Love starts with you.**

—Daily inspiration by Kimi Avary, MA, Relationship Navigation Specialist

4.

Beauty

Beauty is a powerful thing. It stirs us. Calls something out in us. Something deep and true that breaks through the fog of everyday living. It has been said that beauty has the power to elevate even the most mundane things.

I got a taste of this recently. It was early morning, and the usually bustling streets were quiet save the men out watering the lamppost hanging baskets. My husband and I were enjoying a walk through town in the stillness of those early hours.

When we saw the first vase, we both stopped to comment, noting that it was a thoughtful thing for someone to do. Someone left fresh flowers next to a corner bench!

As we rounded the corner, we saw more sweet paper-wrapped bundles of flowers that had been intentionally left in shop doorways or near benches. Bundles and vases were placed all over downtown. Many of them had encouraging handwritten notes attached.

We were so inspired by this little invasion of beauty and thoughtfulness. This small, intentional act of bringing beauty into the everyday set a tone for our day.

So, dear friend, let me ask you: Are you taking the time to see beauty tucked away throughout your day? How are you choosing to leave beautiful imprints on the world around you?

—*Daily inspiration by Shannon McKee, Author, Mentor, and Life Coach*

5.

Thought for the Day

"You came to RADIATE the fullness of who you are."

—ABRAHAM HICKS

6.

Kindness Is Cumulative

Sometimes, it seems like little acts of kindness don't make a difference. It may seem to have zero impact personally or in our communities. Can simply smiling or holding a door open for someone really change the world?

As individual acts, obviously not. If one person in a year does something nice for you, it isn't going to change your outlook on life much. However, if we consistently say kind words, smile, and perform even little acts of kindness, we'll all live in a world that is predominantly pleasant. **Kindness will build cumulatively upon itself and permeate our lives**.

"Constant kindness can accomplish much. As the sun makes ice melt, kindness causes misunderstanding, mistrust, and hostility to evaporate."

—ALBERT SCHWEITZER

—Daily inspiration by Patrick P. Long, International Best-Selling Author

7.

Stop Being the Best Kept Secret

This is your year. You are a beautiful, generous, gifted person who might be someone *that not many people know about* (meaning, a best-kept secret).

Are you top of mind for those people who need your positive impact? Can they easily find you, see you, and hear you?

These are important questions to answer because I've discovered that if they cannot see you and hear you, then you cannot help them. This is why I believe **visibility is so very important** so that it's easy for people to find you.

This is also true: **There is no one out there who is magically going to put you on a stage, and then all your dreams are going to come true.** If you want to make a difference, you have to lead your own effort. If your visibility is low, then it's up to you to raise it—not anyone else but you.

The people who need your positive impact are waiting for you because *you are needed!* Believe me; people need you! People are hurting. People are discouraged. People are losing hope. People are praying and dreaming for somebody just like you to share with them your love, insight, wisdom, and powerful gifts.

Can you make a commitment today to make yourself visible? To shine brightly enough so that your people can see your loving hand outstretched to help them?

Yes! No more hiding!

—Daily inspiration by Rebecca Hall Gruyter, Influencer and Empowerment Leader

8.

Thought for the Day

Love the giver more than the gift.

—BRIGHAM YOUNG

9.

Accept Yourself, Love Yourself!

*"No amount of self-improvement can make
up for any lack of self-acceptance."*

—ROBERT HOLDEN

During this month of love, we easily show love for others. Do we celebrate love for ourselves as easily?

Aspects of *self*-love include *self*-acceptance, *self*-acknowledgment, and *self*-awareness. These are not *self*ish acts. Kindness to yourself is a form of loving self-acceptance. If you aren't kind and loving to yourself first, how can you model love to your teen, family, friends, or colleagues? Trust that when you prioritize yourself, others will learn to value you and themselves more.

The choice is yours to practice self-love or to bully yourself with negative self-talk. You are always in control of two things: your responses and your mindset. You are never in control of other people's actions or words about you, but you are in control of your own thoughts about yourself.

Another aspect of self-love is gratitude. Practice gratitude for yourself on a daily basis for the next thirty days. Journal at least one thing about you that you are grateful for—as simple as appreciating your body for supporting you, your open-mindedness, or tackling a task you've been avoiding. Acknowledge what you have created each day—perhaps a new accomplishment or a way of interacting with others with patience, grace, non-judgment, or respect when in a difficult situation.

Celebrate your self-love! Treat yourself to a massage, a warm bath, a hike in nature, or adding beauty to the world by planting flowers and expressing your creativity.

—Daily inspiration by Dr. Kimberly Schehrer, Teen Breakthrough Expert

10.

Bank on This

If you're finding it impossible to bloom and *shine* because you can't break free from fear, I've written today's message, especially *for you*. In fact, consider yourself gently hugged as you read this because I've been there, too! That's why today I'm sharing **my number-one, simple yet powerful strategy to help release your fear and hold on to your joy.** If you're ready to free yourself from worry that prevents you from taking action and being seen, I invite you to please steal this strategy.

Imagine, for a moment, a high-flying trapeze artist as she prepares to let go of her current reality (the tightly held bar in her hand) so she can reach for the new bar waiting in front of her. **Focus** is her strength and keeps her safe.

In the same way, I invite you to bank on this extraordinary *free* tool: the power of *focus*! The best way to transform your fear into courage is to stay centered in *love* as if your life depends on it because it does. The number-one greatest fear holding you back from achieving your financial dream (or any other dream) is *fear* itself. Remember: you're not alone! Freedom to bloom and *shine* is well within your reach. *Choose* the power that already exists within you to keep fear in perspective. Concentrate *higher, deeper, longer, leaner, wider*, and focus all of your attention on *love*.

—Daily inspiration by Marlene Elizabeth, author of Moneywings™

11.

Thought for the Day

"Let all that you do be done in love."

—1 CORINTHIANS 16:14

12.

Thought for the Day

"When we love, we always strive to become better than we are. When we strive to become better than we are, everything around us becomes better too."

—PAULO COELHO, THE ALCHEMIST

13.

Spend Time with You

"To fall in love with yourself is the first secret to happiness."
—ROBERT MORLEY

This month usually pushes us to examine the relationships in our lives. It is, after all, the month of love. The first step is discovering how to love ourselves and how important that can be. Make that your mission. **Spend time with you. Get to know yourself and fall in love with you.** That is the commencement of true happiness.

—Daily inspiration by Dr. Sarah Breen

14.

Dare to Stand Out

"Do not go where the path may lead, go instead where there is no path and leave a trail."

—RALPH WALDO EMERSON

There is safety in conformity. There is safety in the shadows. There is safety in being like everyone else, for if we stand out, we run the risk of being noticed and being rejected.

Be unique. Take the path not traveled. Stand out from the crowd. All require taking a risk. With great risk could come pain and heartache, as well as perhaps our greatest lessons yet. Stand up. Make your voice heard. Dare to stand out. Risk being you. Know that everyone may not yet be ready for your authentic you. You are. That is enough.

Leadership is about having the courage to be first; **perfection is not required**. Being first is simple. It is not easy. Have the courage to take the first step. Know that others will follow. I can't wait to see you shine!

—Daily inspiration by Dr. Cheryl Lentz, The Academic Entrepreneur

15.

Shine Brightly in the World

What does shine brightly in the world mean to you?

For me, it starts with choosing what I believe in and for what I'm shining. With that clarity, I can then create the boundaries and support that will help me to stand firm and lift others up to move things in a positive direction.

I bring this clarity to my personal life and also to my business life. For me, the two are not separate from each other. For me, my business is part of my way of life.

What could shining brightly mean for your business (and life)? Could it mean:

In every conversation, you allow the opportunity to lift up, support, and really listen to others, whether it's a sales conversation or any other kind.

You continue to move forward with confidence and power on opportunities in the ways you are being called to serve.

You make a choice to be positive and forward-thinking, to be generous with your connections, introductions, and how you serve. This is abundance thinking that is not competitive.

You show up, share your time and skills, help society and the economy move forward (keep the energy of money circulating), even and especially in challenging times.

You feel good about yourself, satisfied with, and gratified by how you have been a bright light today.

How are you choosing to shine each day, in each conversation, and in each opportunity?

—Daily inspiration by Rebecca Hall Gruyter, Influencer and Empowerment Leader

16.

Love and Loss

As February comes to pass each year, I focus my reflections on the romance for which I long—the love we celebrate with warm-colored poetry. I remind myself not of passionate moments in sacred settings, recalling rather brief moments when we feel like the value of money no longer describes our wealth. Moments when a candlelit meal or a plush toy pierced a smile that reminds me of why I fought so hard to find her.

I reflect upon moments when she held my hand while the gasps of words were left cracking like fire embers, and my voice trembled in the footnotes of my deepest doubt-filled reconstruction.

February doesn't last long enough for doubt to cripple you.

Instead, February lasts long enough to remind us the past was real, reminding us of the seconds that we felt would last forever. The ones we then spend years of our lives chasing, so eager to repeat.

In February, I'm grateful for my heartbreaks, as they built my strength of character, helping me believe life is worth living, even when it hurts.

I celebrate those magnificent feelings that we often take for granted, that we leave written in greeting card letters of softness.

In February, I am grateful for the lessons and moments I have been gifted.

May you treasure moments of deep connection, past, present, and yet to come. You were made to connect deeply with others. Be willing to share the gift of you.

—*Daily inspiration by Leigh Bursey, Musician, Speaker, and Municipal Councillor*

17.

Thought for the Day

*"Let us always meet each other with smile,
for the smile is the beginning of love."*

—MOTHER THERESA

18.

Lift Others Up

On January 24, 2020, my husband was given six months to live due to cancer. Immediately, we went to the funeral home, and he planned everything and paid for the funeral. It ended up going faster.

Tony wanted me to move forward with ease when he died. He shared his thoughts on our cars and the house, and he even researched retirement communities for me to buy a smaller house and have money to live. He was proactive in thinking about others and helping us move forward powerfully, even as he faced his last few months.

Tony always surprised me with things he thought would make me happy. A lottery scratch-off ticket, or a plush velour sweater because it was turquoise, my favorite color. He always found a way to lift up others.

Although Tony was extremely sick, he made sure there was a Valentine's gift for me. I sometimes thought he wasn't paying attention, but surprised me often. For a couple of years, I have been doing jigsaw puzzles on my phone. He surprised me with an iPad just to do my puzzles. He was like a little child watching me open my gift. He found great joy in surprising others.

I admired how, even in his last few months, he still found ways to surprise others and lift them up.

How can you lift up someone in your life today? A surprise? How can you encourage them or support them?

—*Daily inspiration by Catherine M. Laub, Podcast Host*

19.

Thought for the Day

"Forget about the fast lane. If you really want to fly, just harness your power to your passion."

—OPRAH WINFREY

20.

Blossom

"And the day came when the risk [it took] to remain tight in the bud was more painful than the risk it took to bloom."

—ANAIS NIN

What if all the effort you have been expending to keep yourself small is part of you growing into your gifts? And something shifts, and you come to realize that you are safe, strong, and have evolved into a brilliant shining light in the world. At a certain point, the bud must bloom to fulfill its destiny.

I invite you to consider all the lessons you have learned from your many life experiences, and consequently, all the ways you have blossomed because of those lessons. Every day we are presented with opportunities to shine as the extraordinary human beings we are designed to be.

I grew up in a small farming community, and my whole world was a five-mile radius of family, friends, home, school, and church. Later, an old married lady of thirty-five, our family of three moved well away from that little cocoon because of my husband's employment status. I used those moves as an opportunity to step into my potential as a leader within our immediate family as well as our new community.

How have you blossomed after life forced you to move beyond the bud?

—Daily inspiration by Mary E. Knippel, Writer Unleashed

21.

Thought for the Day

*"When one door of happiness closes, another opens;
but often we look so long at the closed door that we
do not see the one which has been opened for us."*

—HELEN KELLER

22.

Discover Your Purpose

Seeking fulfillment requires understanding who you are as a promise. Ask yourself and answer the question, "Who am I?" People answer this question with something like "I am Selena," but think of "Selena" as a promise. Because promises are fulfilled in the future, you must envision your ideal self, playing multiple roles in this society, representing a set of values, and giving in abundance to the world. **What roles do you see yourself playing in your environment?** Are you a true friend for those in need of friendship, a mother for those in need of motherhood, or an exceptional guitar player, pianist, or singer? What are the values that you identify with or that best identify you? Are you graceful, kind, honest, respectful, and patient? **Imagine blooming and shining in all your splendid multiple roles and values in this society. There lies the key to the promises that rest latent in you and are waiting to be unleashed toward fulfillment.** Embarking on this journey toward self-fulfillment is noble; see yourself, in the end, radiating beauty, joy, peace, and harmony all around you. With a pen and paper, write an inventory of statements describing who you are in every possible role you see yourself playing. Write something like, "I am a mother for those in need of motherhood," or, "I am kind, graceful, honest, and sincere." Take this role and value inventory of your ideal self and stick a copy everywhere, including your bathroom mirror. Look at it every day as a reminder. You are needed and a beautiful promise to the world.

—*Daily inspiration by Fabien W. Edjou, Author & Life Coach*

23.

Thought for the Day

"Definiteness of purpose is the starting point of all achievement."

—W. CLEMENT STONE

24.

Be Still

I long to be a person of excellence, with knowledge and wisdom. I desire a perfect family, even when it's not perfect. I find love and communication make it perfect enough. I want that relationship where my heart skips a beat. I want what life can offer, even when circumstances aren't going as planned. Stop, slow down, and take a moment to enjoy the best intimate times of your life—moments with God and in nature.

Take the time to open your heart and share your secret thoughts in the stillness of beauty in nature. Listen to God, and you will hear His gentle reply. In the quietness of the outdoor world, if you can be still for a moment, improve your quality of life by listening, looking, and receiving. **There is healing when you open your heart to God and nature.** In the beautiful classroom called nature it teaches many simple yet invaluable lessons where we can gain wisdom and understanding of life. The clouds, in breathtaking formation, yield creative ideas; the bright beams from the sun assure certainty, and the vivid colors of sunset give way to love and romance.

God and nature give hope, peace in the storm, a source of strength, and confidence. When you stay and listen, the voice can be heard; when you distant yourself, the voice is lost before it ever reaches you.

"Be still and know that I am God"

—PS. 46:10).

Receive this moment of being still supported.

—Daily inspiration by Toni Stone Bruce, Precious Stones 4 Life, LLC

25.

Thought for the Day

It's not whether you get knocked down.
It's whether you get up.

– VINCE LOMBARD

26.

Find Your Voice

We are all born with our own unique story—one only we can tell. Find your voice. We are all waiting to hear your story.

—Daily inspiration by Maureen Ryan Blake, Founder and Principal of The Power of the Tribe

27.

Thought for the Day

"Where there is love there is life."

—MAHATMA GANDHI

28.

Walk Through Your Fear

To support us in stepping through our fear, I find tapping into our "why" to be powerfully motivating when I face my fear. Here are the steps I go through to walk through it.

1. **Stop. Pause. Explore what I'm afraid of.**

Feel the feeling, but then explore why it's important to me that I step through it, that I don't let the feeling of fear stop me.

How can I set myself up for success in this situation? What can I do to help me feel safer and supported as I step into this new space? Is it getting support? Is it giving myself permission to leave if I need to?

Take action and lean in and step forward—even if it's a first small step.

I find every time I survive stepping into a new level, my muscle grows stronger, I gain more strength, and eventually, I'm able to soar in that space—and then discover another level that can be stepped into!

Each step prepares you for the next, and you get to build the muscles and strength more visibly on the journey, one step at a time. What step can you take today?

—Daily inspiration by Rebecca Hall Gruyter, Influencer and Empowerment Leader

March

1.

Wired to Serve

Moving forward on your mission doesn't always mean saying *yes* to every opportunity. You have a choice at any time to say *no*—or even better—*not yet.*

When I say *yes* to something, I know I'm saying *no* to something else I may not even know about yet.

Think about that for a moment. This means that with each opportunity that comes my way, I really want to make sure that **it is the way I am called to serve at the highest level.** And there is no one way to do this; it varies with the type of people we are as well as where we are in our life's journey. We are all wired differently.

We can serve our whole lives in important, fulfilling ways without trying to fit ourselves into a box that isn't in alignment with who we are, who we want to be, or what we value.

What I have found is that **you must be willing to be seen on the same level that you want to serve.** If they can't see us, then we can't help those we are called to serve. Discover where your people are and go to them. Be on the platforms they are on, the events they are at, and the circles in which they participate.

—**Daily inspiration by Rebecca Hall Gruyter, Influencer and Empowerment Leader**

2.

A New Season

"No winter lasts forever; no spring skips its turn."
—HAL BORLAND

The change of seasons is coming. You can feel it in the air. Moods start to shift even before the weather. I am excited about this new season. Are you ready for new smells and sounds? Hope is in the air. Are you ready for new beauty to emerge? What are you looking forward to this spring?

—Daily inspiration by Dr. Sarah Breen

3.

Thought for the Day

"Patience, persistence and perspiration make an unbeatable combination for success."

—NAPOLEON HILL

4.

Angelic Communications

I always loved angels, and now I communicate with them. When I'm not doing readings, I am hearing them, and they are always giving me messages. I will hear a song play, and it will be an answer to a question I asked or something they want me to think about. I also see images that jump out at me, and I can relate to the message. They are working with the universe setting things up in my path and helping me along my journey.

The most common sign from a loved one is a shiny penny or dime. Others are feathers, ladybugs, dragonflies, and repeating numbers. They will be in your dreams, and you may feel them by your side.

Everyone receives messages like these. **You need an open mind and to pay attention to what is going on around you. These are not coincidences; they are your loved ones letting you know they are around.**

My husband died in February, and he "plays" songs for me. He loved Neil Diamond, so the first time I asked him to play Neil Diamond, the very next song was what I asked for! Now he sends me many love songs in a row.

Ask your loved one for a specific sign, then watch for it. What message, encouragement, or direction did you receive?

—*Daily inspiration by Catherine M. Laub, Podcast Host*

5.

Celebrate Change

Winter comes with snow and ice, cold temperatures, dreary skies, and hurling winds. A battle has taken place with nature, and it is scheduled for a change and a new beginning. Seeds lay still, waiting for their time. Trees are bare, waiting for their time to bloom. A fragrance of change hints spring is in the air. Reality embraces change positively and steadily. **Nature has no fear. It celebrates each day and a new tomorrow. So why are we fearful and afraid of change? Change only means doing something different.**

We must train and discipline our minds to evaluate what we think, rather than concentrate on what we can't or shouldn't do. We can choose to continually recognize that change will take place. Frequently there is a need for change and growth. Growth requires courage. Changes will come about in life, and we can't avoid it. Instead of resisting change, which will make our lives more difficult, we can choose to acknowledge it, and, in fact, embrace it. Changes in life give one an opportunity to grow and expand. **Fear of change keeps you from being true to yourself.** Fear of change will never allow you to become that person of outstanding achievement, nor have a character balanced with satisfaction and worthiness. Being afraid of change can keep you from reaching goals and the road to happiness.

It's time to celebrate life, its changes, and its discovery. It's time to begin now.

—*Daily inspiration by Toni Stone Bruce, Precious Stones 4 Life, LLC*

6.

Thought for the Day

"I'm a success today because I had a friend who believed in me and I didn't have the heart to let him down."

—ABRAHAM LINCOLN

7.

Thought for the Day

"Don't be pushed around by the fears in your mind. Be led by the dreams in your heart."

—ROY T. BENNETT, THE LIGHT IN THE HEART

8.

Revaluate and Readjust

With March comes the growing pains of revaluation. As spring looms closer, our hunger for it grows, but often so does our realization that our resolutions might require tweaking.

In March, I am grateful for the period of readjustment. The lull before the true journey begins. After all of our hopeful preparations have turned ideas and aspirations into motions. When our cautious optimisms for the warmer weather and our rejuvenations are confronted with our first setbacks and our courses of action are altered.

In March, I am grateful for the ability to change course where needed and rewrite the goals I choose to conquer.

In March, we can inspire ourselves through self-evaluation and affirmation that we are already moving forward.

Be willing to adjust your course as needed to bring your goals forward.

In March, I am thankful for many challenging moments of clarity. May you find clarity and that next step to support you on your journey.

—Daily inspiration by Leigh Bursey, Musician, Speaker, and Municipal Councillor

9.

Be Seen

"Authenticity is a collection of choices that we have to make every day... The choice to let ourselves be seen."

—DR. BRENE BROWN

March is our month to celebrate women's history, and so it is an excellent opportunity to encourage you to step into your greatness. Wherever you are on your path, now is the perfect time to be your authentic self. To make a choice to be seen as the you that you were born to be. **Life will put obstacles in your path, and it's up to you to choose how you cope and utilize the wisdom you absorb from each authentic choice.**

The first time I really felt I was seen as a writer and as a speaker was when my older brother's children came to me to ask that I write and deliver his eulogy. I've kept a journal since I was eleven, so writing is just part of my nature. Writing about my brother was not a problem. But stand up in church and share what I'd written to describe the life of this man whom I'd known and loved for my entire life? I hesitated. Yet, when a well-meaning cousin encouraged me to just let someone else read it, I wiped my tears, cleared my throat, and said, "No. I'm the only one who can tell this story." By the time I'd finished delivering the eulogy, I had everyone laughing through their tears with a playful image of my brother asleep in the clouds.

I invite you to embrace your choices and stand in the light of your authentic self and be seen.

—*Daily inspiration* by Mary E. Knippel, Writer Unleashed

10.

Failure

"Fail faster, succeed sooner."

—DR. CHERYL LENTZ

No one likes this F-word: failure. Somewhere along the way, failure became a four-letter word with a stigma like no other. Initially, I too avoided failure with a mantra: "Failure is not an option." **In time, I grew to understand and learn failure is the *only* option.** We *only* learn from what we do not know. Failure, however, is not a destination, nor an outcome. Failure is a process. It is *not* who we are. Learn to separate yourself, *the person*, from *the skill* you are trying to master.

If you want to succeed, you need to make friends with failure. Failure is a gift. Success is simply getting up one more time than failure knocked you down. Learn faster.

"Success is not final; failure is not fatal. It is the courage to continue that counts."

—WINSTON CHURCHILL

Learning to fail is a skill like any other. Fail brilliantly. Fail with flair and style, as well as grace and eloquence. Success is yours!

—Daily inspiration by Dr. Cheryl Lentz, The Academic Entrepreneur

11.

Thought for the Day

"The most common way people give up their power is by thinking they don't have any."

—ALICE WALKER

12.

Living On Purpose and With Purpose

Welcome to a new year of your purpose-driven life! What does this actually mean?

Your time, energy, gifts, talents, and resources are precious. Choose how you are going to spend—and share—these precious gifts that make *you* who you are and how you're gifted to show up in this world. Yes, *choose!* You get to choose how to spend them on purpose and with great purpose each and every day. And when you do, you expand them and bring even more meaning to your life and to the world!

How do you do that? Here is a key practice:

Stop, pause, and evaluate the day before you. Look at where you are and where you want to be. Then you can make a plan to get there—for your day, your week, or your month.

Stay intentional and mindful as you do this, knowing you have a choice. Go through your day with this in mind: "I am making choices all day, every day, with mindfulness and purpose."

Choose to move forward with those things that matter most to you.

This simple practice will create a life with more ease, productivity, action, and wonderful things coming back to you. When you are living a purpose-driven life, you are doing this not just for yourself but also for those you are serving and interacting with—your employees, children, family, clients, pets, community.

Can you picture how much more strongly and easily you could show up in those places lovingly and powerfully?

—Daily inspiration by Rebecca Hall Gruyter, Influencer and Empowerment Leader

13.

Prepare Your Soil for Growth

Like in farming, you must prepare your soil. Any seed needs soil to germinate, including yours. The soil in which you must plant your seed of promise for your fulfillment is your surroundings. The tools at your disposal to assist your growth are your thoughts, words, and deeds. Your surroundings are made of other people, nature, and man-made objects. **You are the architect of your life and master of your destiny; therefore, you must prepare yourself and your surroundings for the new you.** Everything in your surroundings can add or take away from your value to your life. This means there are people and objects within your surroundings that add value to your life and others that don't. **Be mindful of what and who you surround yourself with.** Your task in preparing your soil consists of identifying the people and object that adds value to your life and then cutting off everything else. **The farmer doesn't play around with weeds that can potentially hinder the growth of his crop; he removes them.** Your tools—meaning thoughts, words, and deeds—can either be positive or negative. **To succeed in this journey, positivity is your secret weapon.** Being positive and only investing your energy in the people and things that add value to your life are the secret ingredients for your march toward success. **What that means is think, talk, and act positively.**

—Daily inspiration by Fabien W. Edjou, Author & Life Coach

14.

Thought for the Day

"Success is getting what you want,
happiness is wanting what you get."

—INGRID BERGMAN

15.

Happiness

"You know why it's hard to be happy—it's because we refuse to let go of the things that make us sad."

—BRUCE H. LIPTON, THE BIOLOGY OF BELIEF

"Nothing can bring you happiness if you are not already filled with the capacity for it."

—KIMI AVARY, MA, RELATIONSHIP NAVIGATION SPECIALIST

Are you unhappy? Are you waiting for the magic pill that will make all your sadness and unhappiness go away? Do you expect someone outside yourself to make you happy? Sadly, there is no magic pill, and no one is capable of making you happy. **In order to be happy, you have to allow yourself to be happy. You have to choose to be happy for no reason. That's right. Happiness is an inside job.** No one outside yourself can ever truly make you happy. They can contribute to your happiness, but they cannot do it for you. Sometimes we are afraid to let ourselves show happiness because we think if we do, whatever good is happening will vanish. So we hold back expressing our happiness waiting for that perfect moment when the stars are aligned to let it out. It doesn't work that way. You cannot get to that burst of joy at the pinnacle unless your happiness muscle has been worked. You must first choose to let yourself be happy. You must let your heart discover the essence of happiness within yourself. Pause and reach inside yourself and discover where happiness lives inside you.

—Daily inspiration by Kimi Avary, MA, Relationship Navigation Specialist

16.

A Prevalence of Good

It can seem overwhelming watching the news or focusing on current events, and we can feel that everything around us is falling apart. Negative things are always happening in the world, but these are sensationalized in the media, and most good news is ignored. If we look at the big picture and focus on human history, a much different pattern becomes apparent.

Overall, life has improved, and societies have progressed consistently over time. This demonstrates the prevalence of good in the world around us. If the bad in people outweighed the good, we would have destroyed ourselves long ago, and progress would have been impossible. This illustrates that humans are predominantly good, and that applies to you and nearly everyone around you. **Embrace it and let the good flourish. Project kindness to others and accept it graciously in return.**

We can easily see how far we have progressed. Technology, infrastructure, medicine, and more have evolved to levels beyond what most people could have even imagined centuries ago, and we have utilized these advancements to improve our lives. **As we focus on the good and continue to contribute to our communities in positive ways, we continue to foster a better world and a greater good.**

Darkness is merely the absence of light, and the sun is always shining. The light never yields to the dark. Whenever light is present, it is always the darkness that yields.

"Even the darkest night will end and the sun will rise."

—VICTOR HUGO

—Daily inspiration by Patrick P. Long, International Best-Selling Author

17.

Moving Forward

Have you (or a loved one) endured a long, painful battle (financial, physical, emotional, spiritual, or in a relationship), and it's only now just sinking in that the storm is finally over? Perhaps you find yourself wondering, "Now what?" as you nurse your wounds and pick up the broken pieces. If so, I invite you to ask yourself the following gentle question:

What seed can I plant right now, so it takes root and blooms in my life three months from now? What seed might you choose to plant?

Self-care?

Family and friendship time?

An emergency savings fund?

A new job or business?

Weight loss?

A new residence?

A vacation?

Financial independence?

Your mission—if you choose to accept it—is for the next twelve weeks, **water, feed, protect,** and **shine a light on** the seed you plant in your life.

Determine a mini action-step you can take *today* in any one of the categories above (or whatever priority is essential to you) that will set you up to experience a *win* (big or small) ninety days from now.

Remember to celebrate your achievement when you reach your goal *and also each day and week* as you nurture that important seed in your life. Not only will you experience the necessary sunshine you need regularly, but also gain confidence, strength, and joy from the delicious fruit of your labor.

—Daily inspiration by Marlene Elizabeth, author of Moneywings™

18.

Thought for the Day

*"Efforts and courage are not enough
without purpose and direction."*

—JOHN F. KENNEDY

19.

Spring Forward and *Shine*!

"You can have roots and wings."

—JAKE, IN SWEET HOME ALABAMA

There's something about a seed knowing what it is and what it's going to become. It starts digging its roots in deep so that it can grow and shine as it's made to do. That describes us as well! We can lean into who we truly are, what we truly need, and who we are truly made to be. Sometimes it's hidden deep down under old stories and messages we've received, but we are gifted to serve with all our unique talents, abilities, and dreams, just like the rose has been gifted with color, scent, delicate petals, and strong stems.

I believe you "can have roots and wings," as Jake says in the movie ***Sweet Home Alabama***. **In fact, we *need* both to *shine*.** We have roots that we send down deep into the earth, a foundation for the actions that will support us in bringing forward what we are called to do and be. Our roots are our plans, our talents, our resources, and the loving people who support us. Our deep roots help us weather the storms of life as we grow and blossom.

We also have wings—dreams, goals, callings—that pull us to fly! Our wings take us to new opportunities to *shine* and to light the path for others. We're able to spring forward to *shine* because we have our roots to support us.

Today, let's celebrate our roots and our wings and all the gifts we've been given to share! **Let your roots go deep, and your wings give flight to your dreams, passion, and purpose.**

—Daily inspiration by Rebecca Hall Gruyter, Influencer and Empowerment Leader

20.

It Is Not About Me

When I become uncertain or distracted, I just remind myself, "It is not about me." It is about the people I have been chosen to serve. This supports me to shift and get back on track.

So remember, it's not about you but about those you serve.

—Daily inspiration by Maureen Ryan Blake, Founder and Principal of The Power of the Tribe

21.

Thought for the Day

"Act as if it was, and it will be."

—LAILAH GIFTY AKITA, PEARLS OF WISDOM: GREAT MIND

22.

Show All Your Colors as You Bloom

There's joy in discovery, in showing up, in shining, in stretching to a new, exciting place.

In my own journey, I resisted being visible; I wanted to disappear. What have I discovered in being willing to be seen, going through being vulnerable, stripping away some of the layers I'd been hiding behind, and really being seen exactly as I am?

It is actually freeing and joyful. I discovered that the "old way"—of acting a certain way, hiding parts of myself, following others' rules—takes a lot of energy. It drains our life away. And people can't really connect with us because we are not fully ourselves. **When we are willing to strip all that away and say, "This is me!" our energy increases, and people really lean in and connect. What joy that brings to everyone!**

Feeling joy and fun ties up all the other parts like a beautiful gift box. It keeps us remembering who we are, how colorful we are, what a wonderful light we shine. Laughter and joy are present-moment experiences that bring everyone together. How can you share more of yourself?

—Daily inspiration by Rebecca Hall Gruyter, Influencer and Empowerment Leader

23.

Thought for the Day

"Shine like a rising Sun."

—LAILAH GIFTY AKITA

24.

Mondays

Sometimes Mondays are hard. Sometimes your daughter has a bumpy start (which usually means you have a bumpy start). And the laundry piles high from a busy weekend. And your schedule gets set a little off-kilter. And your loose-leaf tea is too pulverized, so you get little bits of tea floating out of the tea ball into your mug. And you remember that you forgot to plan the menu because you took a nap Sunday afternoon instead, so there's no real plan for feeding your family dinner tonight. And maybe your to-do list feels a bit too long. And you read the news when you should have been making the bed. It was more political mayhem, making you feel grumpy inside.

No, is it just me? Is it just me who needs a pause on Monday? To remember author Ann Voskamp's words that "life change comes when we receive life with thanks and ask for nothing to change." Her words remind me to receive it all with thanks. All of life. Not just the stuff that's easy to receive, like the sun on my face or my favorite hoodie or the lingering hug from a loved one. But all of it – even the bumpy starts.

What would it be like to turn Monday on its head and dare to live fully right where you are?

—*Daily inspiration by Shannon McKee, Author, Mentor, and Life Coach*

25.

Thought for the Day

"I never dreamed about success. I worked for it."

—ESTEE LAUDER

26.

Are You Ready to Let Go and Be Empowered?

"It's never too late to be who you might have been."
—GEORGE ELIOT

To me, empowerment means to feel mastery over your life, choices, and results. You feel confident to freely express yourself, the self-worth to create the life you desire, and passion for contributing to change in your world.

What takes away your power?

Thinking about this helps you identify what the opposite, or empowered, would look like. It might be not feeling in alignment with your values, not living up to your standards and within your boundaries, sacrificing yourself to please others, or being afraid to take an action step that would improve your life.

How can you feel more empowered?

This is a terrific process to do for yourself or with your teen, giving yourself and/or them the permission to consider how they might lead a more fulfilling life. To help find the answer, take some time to ground yourself, and bring yourself to a state of presence. Then contemplate this question:

What are you holding onto that if you let go, would shift your life?

Be aware of what feelings, thoughts, and "Aha" moments come up for you. Consider what comes up with kindness to yourself; there's no wrong answer. Then ask yourself if you are **willing to surrender that story, what you are holding onto, so that you can move forward in the future you'd like to create.**

Remember, sometimes, it takes more courage to let go than it does to hold on. And it's never too late.

—Daily inspiration by Dr. Kimberly Schehrer, Teen Breakthrough Expert

27.

Thought for the Day

"Power is not given to you. You have to take it."

—BEYONCE KNOWLES

28.

Thought for the Day

*"One is loved because one is loved.
No reason is needed for loving."*

—PAULO COELHO, THE ALCHEMIST

29.

Choose to Shine

"The more you shine, the more you are paving the way for others."

—REBECCA HALL GRUYTER

I'm passionate about empowering women and men because I know firsthand what it's like to come from a much-disempowered place. I experienced all types of abuse during my most formative years. This environment of abuse made me believe false messages like I am not okay; there is something wrong with me, and that it is *not* safe to be seen or heard.

As a result, I became an expert in hiding. When I was finally rescued, I was able to start my healing journey. I discovered that these beliefs I had embraced all those years were actually lies. **I discovered that I am beautifully and wonderfully made, and so are you! I discovered that I matter and am needed just as I am—and that it is safe to be seen, heard, and shine. The same is true for you, too!**

It became my mission (and it still is!) to help others understand these same truths. My life and work have taken me to places I could never have dreamed of, reaching thousands of people all over the world with my message because I have chosen to *shine.*

When you share the amazing gift of *you*, the more you shine, and the more you pave the way for others to shine, too! How can you share more of yourself and *shine* (share) the fit of you with the world?

—Daily inspiration by Rebecca Hall Gruyter, Influencer and Empowerment Leader

30.

Thought for the Day

"A friend is one that knows you as you are, understands where you have been, accepts what you have become, and still, gently allows you to grow. "

—WILLIAM SHAKESPEARE

31.

Step Into Your Visibility

My work is about helping experts overcome fear so they can bring their message forward to help the world be a better place. Here are three ways to make this shift to being more visible:

Be *willing* to be seen. We must be willing to be seen on the same level that we are to serve. In other words, if we want to serve, we must allow others to get to know who we are and how we can serve them. You can't help them if they can't see and hear you.

Dance *with* the fear. Fear is an emotion that rises when you are stepping into a new space, and your body isn't sure if it's safe yet. Your fear is trying to protect you. In truth, you are not in danger, so you can assure your emotions that what you are feeling is discomfort simply because you are doing something that you haven't ever done before and been willing to feel the emotion and step forward anyway.

Remember your "why"—the reason you are stepping forward into visibility is to serve more people, to meet a need in the world that you are uniquely qualified and called to do. Your why will always be there to inspire and motivate you to step forward powerfully, even when you're afraid.

I can't wait to see you shine!

—*Daily inspiration by Rebecca Hall Gruyter, Influencer and Empowerment Leader*

April

1.

Thought for the Day

"Life is like a coin. You can spend it any way you wish, but you only spend it once."

—LILLIAN DICKSON

2.

Thought for the Day

"Be patient with yourself. Self-growth is tender; it's holy ground. There's no greater investment."

—STEPHEN COVEY

3.

Breathe Deeper

The first-quarter earnings have been calculated. Taxes filed, and business is as usual. Spring rains arrive to wash away the grit and grime of salt-stained automobiles. The air is still crisp. The temperature is still confused. And so often in these moments, we feel compelled to feel frustrated. We illustrate our agonies by giving up on goals and drowning in our temperament.

This is the moment in our stories when we remember to breathe deeper and let the moisture of the springtime dawn fill our longing lungs. This renewal is beyond a fresh scented memory or the sounds of heavy hail colliding with the tin roofs of our hearts.

As the sparrows and the robins sing their morning symphonies in April, I am inspired to taste greater hope, health, and purpose. May you take deeper breaths, pause, and remember your greatness.

In April, I welcome the sounds of mornings worth waking up for.

—*Daily inspiration by Leigh Bursey, Musician, Speaker, and Municipal Councillor*

4.

Thought for the Day

"Money and success don't change people; they merely amplify what is already there."

—WILL SMITH

5.

Bloom

"You don't get to choose how you're going to die. Or when.
You can only decide how you're going to live. Now."

—JOAN BAEZ

Are you feeling stagnant or stuck in your life? It may be that you've let yourself be influenced by others and the world around you more than you were guided by your internal wisdom. **This is your life!** That may sound obvious, but sometimes we feel like our lives are beyond our control. We feel like we are victims of the people and circumstances around us. Bronnie Ware, a palliative caregiver, listened to her patients as they were coming to the end of their lives. What she heard over and over again was that people wished they had had the courage to live the life they had wanted. They wished that they hadn't worked so hard, that they had expressed their feelings, that they had stayed in touch with friends, and that they had had the courage to let themselves be happier. **Every day, ask yourself, if I were to die tomorrow, will I regret not having done the dream that's in my heart? Will I regret not having called someone let them know I care about them, let them know how I feel, or to make amends? Will I regret not sharing my story and passions with the world? Will I regret not choosing to be happy regardless of circumstances? What shift in my perception is needed to savor every moment and allow me to bloom?**

—*Daily inspiration by Kimi Avary, MA, Relationship Navigation Specialist*

6.

Thought for the Day

"Could anything be better than this Waking up every day knowing that lots of people are smiling because you chose to impact lives, making the world a better place."

—ANYAELE SAM CHIYSON

7.

Unapologetically You

"Every woman deserves one place that is unapologetically hers."
—JACQUELINE DE MONTRAVEL

When you think of one place that is unapologetically your own, do you go to a cozy chair by a sunny window with fragrant flowerpots and birds chirping outside? Are you in a lounge chair beside the pool or ocean? Perhaps a booklined study with a deep comfy couch and a roaring fire?

These are all wonderful options. And I hope if they are not physically part of your world, they may now exist in your imaginary escapes from your daily life.

May I propose another place easily within your reality and most definitely unapologetically your own? It will not take up much real estate and is absolutely portable. Are you intrigued?

I'm talking about one place that has been my companion, confidant, counselor, and soul sister since I was eleven years old.

Have you guessed yet?

My journal is the one place that is unapologetically my own!

Writing in a journal is a way to create your own little world while you explore ways to cope with the dilemmas of your day-to-day life. No special training is required, no expensive equipment or tools necessary. Not even a specific wardrobe to worry about. It's just you showing up on the page to have a conversation on paper.

Imagine the places you could go if you devoted five minutes a day to put your thoughts on paper. It could change your life.

—Daily inspiration by Mary E. Knippel, Writer Unleashed

8.

Thought for the Day

"You must bloom wherever God plants you."

—TANIA SILVA

9.

Value All Relationships

Something I didn't recognize or appreciate until recently is how important even "casual friendships" are. In my younger days, I thought of friendships as either well established or non-existent. It was one or the other. I was friends with someone, or I wasn't.

I've come to understand and appreciate how much "casual friendships" or "occasional relationships" enrich my life. I used to be hurt if someone I felt I connected with didn't invite me to a party or want to spend more time together, but now I've learned to value the time I have with anyone I encounter. I joke and laugh and share stories much more openly and freely with anyone willing to reciprocate kindly and in a friendly manner.

I believe we should embrace even the most fleeting interactions with others, even with random strangers we may never see again. Enjoy the minutes, learn from others, and put a bright little spark in their day. Since I learned to do this, I feel much more connected to my community. I feel like I have friends all around, even casual friends I barely know, who have bright smiles, kind words, quick wits, and uplifting laughs to share and spread. It fills me with a wonderful feeling that kindness and friendship abound in my community and in my world, and I get to experience it so frequently. How can you embrace connections and relationships more deeply and frequently?

—*Daily inspiration by Patrick P. Long, International Best-Selling Author*

10.

Thought for the Day

"I've missed more than 9000 shots in my career. I've lost almost 300 games. 26 times I've been trusted to take the game winning shot and missed. I've failed over and over and over again in my life. And that is why I succeed."

—MICHAEL JORDAN

11.

Spring Forward in Your Relationship with Money

Sometimes we have this "thing" about money. Many people know we have to deal with it, but we'd really rather not have to talk about it; we just hope that everything falls into place.

So we get disconnected from money. We leave money out of the conversation about our intentions, our goals, and our wants, which makes it hard for money to support our intentions, goals, and purpose.

I want to encourage you to instead purposely build a relationship, an ongoing conversation, with money. Let money in on what you want from it! Open your ears; listen to what's being offered to you. You can see what serves you and what does not: What do you really need? What do you want to build and create? What matters to you? Let money be part of what you are looking to build and create: a valued and trusted partner.

Discover how to connect with money, communicate with money, and build what matters most to you with money coming alongside to support you. Remember, money doesn't get to direct the relationship—you get to choose. Choose to build a positive relationship with money.

—Daily inspiration by Rebecca Hall Gruyter, Influencer and Empowerment Leader

12.

Because Life Is a Team Sport

Focus on what you can control. Treat people with dignity, whether you win or lose. Keep your "emotional tank" filled. How you show up in life matters. A simple positive attitude radiates its own kind of *sunshine* into your community, relationships, and life, setting a powerful ripple effect into motion that empowers people to *bloom, shine,* and *grow*—including you. That's why I created a simple exercise for my clients called "**Fifteen Ways to Bloom and Shine, A Simple Daily Meditation to Show Up at Your Best**" (choose one to follow daily, weekly, or monthly):

Today, I will...
Comfort others as I comfort myself.
Be kind to others as I am kind to myself.
Spread joy to others as I create joy for myself.
Forgive others as I forgive myself.
Encourage others as I encourage myself.
Believe in your dreams as I believe in my dreams.
Celebrate your success as I celebrate my success.
Focus on the good in others as I focus on the good in myself.
Appreciate your beauty as I appreciate my beauty.
Respect your values as I respect my values.
Honor your boundaries as I honor my boundaries.
Delight in you as I delight in being me.
Bask in your brilliance as I bask in my brilliance.
Bless you, as I bless myself.
Love you as I love myself.
Watch you bloom, shine, and grow as I experience myself bloom, shine, and grow.
... because life is a team sport.
Amen.

—Daily inspiration by Marlene Elizabeth, author of Moneywings™

13.

Thought for the Day

"Stop limiting your potential. Realize that there's an unlimited amount of things that you can do with your life."

— SONYA PARKER

14.

Polish Your Light to Shine Even Brighter

Periodically, it's important to take some time to step back from the weeds and think about *you*.

Look at what excites you about your business. It may involve reminding yourself of your original mission and purpose in getting into this business. You may discover something that you thought was important at the beginning but is not so important or within your focus now. Notice whether or not you would miss that thing if you released it.

Think about what keeps rising to the top for you—is it something that your customers are asking for consistently? Is it something you're feeling called to do, like speak on stage or write a book? Is it a new direction you can begin to set a vision to achieve down the road in a few months or years? Is it a shift in your role as ambassador of your brand (the "face" of the company)? Are you feeling that your brand could benefit from your taking less of a customer-facing role or a more visible role?

These are all considerations that are important to contemplate, journal about, and maybe discuss with people close to you whom you trust. It's worth the time so that you can be sure you are moving in the right direction with your growth plan.

—Daily inspiration by Rebecca Hall Gruyter, Influencer and Empowerment Leader

15.

Think Big

Mark Twain once said, "Keep away from people who try to belittle your ambitions. Small people always do that, but the really great make you feel that you too can become great."

The earth is full of space, distance, and greatness. Orion, a distinctive constellation, which embraces some of the brightest cluster of stars in the sky, can be seen on a beautiful night around the world. However, this starry grandeur lies approximately 1,360 light-years from planet earth. A huge distance, incomprehensible to the mind. Its light extends far into the galaxy of the starry night sky. Welcome to the universe, to Greatness, our Higher Power, and the source of strength, life, and blessings.

"Believing in the impossible with hard work can create a path of abundance." Think big and believe big. No matter who you may be, and what you may have done, you must see yourself at the finish line. **Don't give up and don't quit on yourself; it is well worth the ride. Have hope and a desire to achieve**. The qualities are in our character, but we must explore and ignite the flames to become better people, above the average. Strength is available to enjoy blessings unlimited. Think and believe it.

What is your big vision? What step can you take to bring it forward? Go pave the way and know that I am lifting you up and cheering you on. I can't wait to see you shine!

—*Daily inspiration by Toni Stone Bruce, Precious Stones 4 Life, LLC*

16.

Let Beauty Germinate from Within

Becoming! Can you notice the transformative power that lies in this word alone? **Becoming means "beginning to be."** Just as the DNA of a fruitful tree is latent and invisible in a seed, so should your DNA to fulfillment be. Note that becoming is also a compound word between "be"

—being) and "coming." **You can clearly see the foundation for the Law of Attraction to be set in motion.** In order to become, you must first be or begin to be the individual that you aspire toward. **In more practical terms, once you start being and acting in thoughts, words, and deed as the ideal individual that you intend to become at the end of this incredible journey, the Law of Attraction is set in motion and attracts all the elements in nature that will allow you to eventually become the manifestation of your vision.** Ride the fresh breeze of spring to sink the roots of the new you firmly in your surroundings, let beauty germinate from within, and watch the new you sprout upward toward luminous heights and ennoblement.

The rain in life creates the magic of loosening the soil for all seeds to crack their coat, sink their root, sprout their first leaves, and thrust their fragile stem upward. **Just as the seed undergoes all these transformations underground, most of your April work is from within and on yourself. May the spring showers loosen any rigidity in you so that your new seed can start its growth and process toward your ideal self.**

—*Daily inspiration by Fabien W. Edjou, Author & Life Coach*

17.

Thought for the Day

And above all these put on love, which binds everything together in perfect harmony.

—COLOSSIANS 3:14

18.

Success

Success is where opportunity and preparedness meet.

Many are credited with such a statement. This is where you have to do your homework. There are no shortcuts. There are no magic wands, no magic carpets. If you want the outcome, if you want the dream, *you need to do the work.* You have to show up and do the work each and every time. Some call this paying your dues.

Be ready to step into your success, prepare, and do your work. Opportunity is all around us. The question is whether or not you will be ready when the call comes. Prepare, so you are. Be ready to say yes and step into your success.

—*Daily inspiration by Dr. Cheryl Lentz, The Academic Entrepreneur*

19.

Thought for the Day

*"Don't be afraid to speak up for yourself.
Keep fighting for your dreams!"*

—GABBY DOUGLAS

20.

Darkness to Light

"The tiny seed knew that in order to grow, it needed to be dropped in dirt, covered with darkness, and struggle to reach the light."

—SANDRA KRING

What an amazing thought! As we think about planting our gardens full of new flowers and vegetables, so too should we consider our personal growth. **Change is scary and sometimes dark, but you must embrace the darkness to someday reach the light.** To evolve as a person, to scale the plateau of your current life, you have to veer from your path. Something must change.

You will probably never "feel" ready to take that leap, ready to be covered with dirt. Who would? Do it anyway. Try something new, and never look back.

—Daily inspiration by Dr. Sarah Breen

21.

Thought for the Day

"The way I see it, if you want the rainbow, you gotta put up with the rain."

—DOLLY PARTON

22.

Overcoming Obstacles and Challenges

For most of the last couple of years, I struggled with many mental illnesses. I was hospitalized many times and always overcame the difficulties. This year alone, I was hospitalized three times.

There were many obstacles and challenges in supporting my husband having a terminal disease.

My husband, Tony, died in February 2020, and I'm left to carry on alone. Since then, my depression is gone, and I'm accomplishing many tasks, where before, I felt stagnant and scattered. I miss Tony dearly and am still grieving. The positive result was my focus and feeling lighter where I can breathe, not feel smothered any more.

The message here is that even though there were many obstacles and challenges, we can overcome them. We can become ready to start a new life and move in a new direction on our journey.

We all have challenges at times. The way we respond and handle them makes the difference between overcoming the situation and turning toward a bad outcome.

Sit still for a short while and think of a challenge you had and journal the positive and negative. How can you move toward a more positive outcome for you and those around you?

—*Daily inspiration by Catherine M. Laub, Podcast Host*

23.

Hold Space

My clients often hear me say, "Hold space" during our coaching calls. It is within this space you allow others grace for them to come into their own as they work to find their purpose. Remember to hold space for yourself and others.

—Daily inspiration by Maureen Ryan Blake, Founder and Principal of The Power of the Tribe

24.

Thought for the Day

"In life you get what you put in. When you make a positive impact in someone else's life, you also make a positive impact in your own life."

—MARCANDANGEL

25.

Pound the Table

"What makes you pound the table?"

It was 1994, and I was just a couple of years out of college. The asker was my boss, and we were sitting in a staff meeting. It was his way of asking us what we really get excited about. It's a truly great question. One that gets at the heart of our passions and the things that move us.

I didn't really know how to answer him. I was twenty-four.

I'd been a people-pleaser for so long that I think I mostly got passionate about whatever I thought people wanted me to get passionate about.

Now, I'm fifty, and I think I'm finally self-aware enough to figure out some of the things that make me jump up out of my seat and pound the table. Things like intentional living; storytelling and soul-stirring moments; beauty and gratitude in every the everyday of life; snapshots of redemption; living in community; hospitality and creating refuge in my home; glimpses of grace this side of heaven; and leaving a legacy of grace through faith.

What about you? Do you know what makes you pound the table? What stirs your soul? How can you cultivate it this week?

—*Daily inspiration by Shannon McKee, Author, Mentor, and Life Coach*

26.

Thought for the Day

"It only takes one person to make you happy and change your life: YOU."

—CHARLES ORLANDO

27.

It's Not Your Job to Please Everybody, Is It?

I discovered that it's not my job to please everybody—it sounds simple, doesn't it? As vulnerable as that might make you feel, know that you cannot step onto center stage as an expert or influencer without taking a stand, and that stand simply won't please everybody!

You know and keep your boundaries and go forward with the awareness that people will say and feel a lot of things about you and your business. **Don't get caught up in what others say. Stay aware and observe where there's truth and where there isn't.**

Take in what will serve your brand, business, and life, and kindly release what will not. One phrase I've found that helps me keep my boundaries is: "I can really see how you feel this way; however, this is what we do here."

Be willing to lead and bring forward all you are called to bring forward. Stand in your truth and shine!

—*Daily inspiration by Rebecca Hall Gruyter, Influencer and Empowerment Leader*

28.

If You Could Not Fail, What Would Be Different?

"F.E.A.R: False Evidence Appearing Real."

—AUTHOR UNKNOWN

It takes courage to take positive risks. Fear has us choosing to continue with familiar patterns to keep us safe and knowing what to expect. However, if our expectations remain the same, then are we truly evolving into our best selves?

To thrive, we must step over the edge of our comfort zone and be adventurous instead of allowing fear or self-doubt to stop us. When you feel fear, it is most often an indication to take that leap of faith and explore another choice.

Fear is often a distraction from choosing an action that is loaded with the potential to soar beyond what we ever imagined possible. Don't quit on you. Ask yourself these questions:

What am I really afraid of?

What does this fear keep me distracted with?

If I knew I could not fail, what would be different?

Allow yourself to experience a different way of being. Then, choose an action that moves you in a new, positive direction.

These are powerful questions to explore yourself and to share with your children/teens to help them better understand how their fears may be holding them back.

—Daily inspiration by Dr. Kimberly Schehrer, Teen Breakthrough Expert

29.

Thought for the Day

"Life is 10% what happens to me and 90% of how I react to it."

—CHARLES SWINDOLL

30.

Delegate

Are you looking to expand and have a bigger impact on your business? It's not something that can be done on your own. When I am at a growth point in my business, I think of my garden—the mint, specifically. It's so beautiful, aromatic, and yummy in a glass of iced tea. Yet, if I'm not careful, it starts to take over my whole yard!

In my business, it's the point at which my tasks and responsibilities seem to be taking over everything and smothering new opportunities and projects like the mint in my garden crowding out other blooms. It's time to delegate. **Here are some tips to get started:**

List the things you need support on and what you would love to hand over and delegate to someone.

If you have a budget to work with, prioritize the work you need to have done and find the people with expertise to do it. Get creative—there are many ways to outsource talent!

Consider trading services—as long as it makes sense for your business and is serving both parties. If you choose to make trades, evaluate them regularly to make sure they are a win-win.

Make these choices sooner than later—*before* your yard is taken over by mint!

What can you start to delegate today to grow your business, impact, and reach?

—*Daily inspiration by Rebecca Hall Gruyter, Influencer and Empowerment Leader*

May

1.

Come Out of Hiding and *Shine*!

This means that **we can't hide behind the roles that we play, our credentials, or our limiting beliefs.** These things (which we believe are protecting us) actually block people from truly hearing and experiencing us—the very people who need us are separated from us.

The only way to be found is for you to be willing to take off all that stuff that is blocking the connection. The only way to truly make a positive difference in the world is to be willing to be seen authentically and transparently.

I invite you today to look at ways in which you might be hiding a little bit. Please do this without self-judgment or criticism and always with self-love.

And then ask: In what ways could I step out of hiding onto the center stage of my life just a little bit more?

A great first step is to decide on an action you could take today to lean into making a difference for another and to shine your light for them.

—*Daily inspiration by Rebecca Hall Gruyter, Influencer and Empowerment Leader*

2.

Thought for the Day

"The best way to predict the future is to create it"

—ABRAHAM LINCOLN

3.

Mother's Day

*"A flower does not think it's competing with
the flower next to it; it just blooms."*

—ANONYMOUS

*"The quickest way to make yourself miserable
is to compare yourself to someone else."*

—KIMI AVARY, MA, RELATIONSHIP NAVIGATION SPECIALIST

It's easy to lose yourself when you're focused on comparing yourself to others. Looking for others to establish your value only serves to deplete your vital life force. It causes anxiety and depression because instead of allowing your inner essence to shine, the message you are sending to yourself is that you are less than these other people. Your soul knows better. Those feelings are a signal that your comparison is not in alignment with your true self. Turn your attention inside yourself and nurture your inner being. Examine your past for gifts. Every experience, no matter how awful, has gifts. When you look, you will find them. These gifts are the seeds for your heart desires. Be grateful for those gifts. Gratitude is a powerful fertilizer for the seeds of your true self. You're not perfect; no one is. Perfection is an illusion. **You are beautiful, just as you are. Be grateful for all that you are right now.** Instead of lamenting where you are in your life, accept what is, and if you want to change something to be more in alignment with your true self, take action. **Let joy guide your choices instead of fear. Choose to allow your inner essence to bloom!**

—Daily inspiration by Kimi Avary, MA, Relationship Navigation Specialist

4.

Thought for the Day

"The most effective way to do it, is to do it."

—AMELIA EARHART

5.

Cultivate Your Garden

Maybe only a few people around you have noticed your internal changes. Pause and celebrate your achievement(s). Alone is the most delicate phase of your transformative journey, the only birthplace of rebirth, away from distractions. This is why it is important to celebrate your growth. Energy drives any empowerment. **You empower everything you give your attention to, whether internally or externally.** Remember, you will reap what you sow; therefore, act as a sieve to balance between giving and receiving. I believe three fundamental conditions must be fulfilled to succeed in your journey:

Purity: You must always give with detachment and pure intentions meaning without expecting anything in return. Being fake or pretending doesn't make the cut. If you are incapable of purity in your intentions, then take all the time necessary to practice and master this.

Love: Genuine love has nothing to do with feelings. Feelings are physical, while love is spiritual and divine because it comes directly from God. Genuine love cares about giving exclusively what is best and will benefit the loved one.

Justice: Justice is inseparable from genuine love; therefore, love is also justice in action. Justice doesn't do favors but treats everyone the same regardless of social affiliations. Justice is also kindness because it doesn't rejoice from the sufferings of others. Just like love, justice only gives what is best.

May you choose to celebrate you and give focus and energy to caring for others deeply and richly. Put your love into action.

—*Daily inspiration by Fabien W. Edjou, Author & Life Coach*

6.

Quiet Peace

My parents live in a rural part of Mississippi. Visiting is always a time of respite. The internet is spotty. The pace is slow. In the evenings, we can sit on the back patio and stare up into a vast sky that is free of light pollution. They drive 40 minutes to the nearest shopping area. The thing is, they wanted this. They chose to build out there, to step away from the constant press of information and engagement and busyness.

We can't all make that radical of a change, but we can all make small choices to push back the noise.

When was the last time you just sat? Still in the moonlight? Or quiet in the moments before dawn? Gave your soul time to breathe? Found yourself weeping at the beauty of music that rises heavenward where words dare not break the mystery of the moment? Left the radio off in your car and let the silence wash over you? What can you do today to reclaim some quiet and stillness?

—Daily inspiration by Shannon McKee, Author, Mentor, and Life Coach

7.

Thought for the Day

You cannot afford to live in potential for the rest of your life; at some point, you have to unleash the potential and make your move.

—ERIC THOMAS

8.

Adversity

"Every adversity, every failure, and every heartache carries with it the seed of an equivalent or greater benefit."

—NAPOLEON HILL

This one takes strength to understand and process. My hope was that in dark times, I could accept challenges with grace, poise, and elegance. It is easy when things go right. It is a test of strength, will, and character when things don't. When the universe gives you such a test, do you pass? Remember, the universe will often give us the opportunity to redo this lesson over and over until we get it right. Simple? Yes. Easy? No. Will you get it right the next time?

Some of our most epic triumphs are in some of our darkest moments. The question is whether we can see the rainbow after the rain. Can we celebrate once we have passed the test? Can we know that doing the right thing is always the right thing to do, even if it is the most difficult thing we have ever done?

We do not grow in our comfort zone. We grow when we are out of our comfort zone. Learning can be painful as a necessary part of the process. We do the work; then, we remain steadfast in the patience needed to reap the benefits of that hard work. **Try not to lose heart. Know that you've got this, and the outcome will be better than anything you could have ever hoped for or imagined. Be patient. Believe.**

—Daily inspiration by Dr. Cheryl Lentz, The Academic Entrepreneur

9.

Thought for the Day

"A woman is like a tea bag – you never know how strong she is until she gets in hot water."

—ELEANOR ROOSEVELT

10.

Thought for the Day

"The only place success comes before work is in the dictionary."

—VINCE LOMBARDI

11.

Connection

It is all about connection.

The greatest resource any truly successful person will say is their network, the trusted people they have aligned and served with during their journey. What connections are you creating, building, and allowing in your life?

—*Daily inspiration by Maureen Ryan Blake, Founder and Principal of The Power of the Tribe*

12.

Thought for the Day

"Your time is limited, so don't waste it living someone else's life. Don't be trapped by dogma – which is living with the results of other people's thinking."

—STEVE JOBS

13.

Communication

Value Communication and Focus on Others

As my wife's battle with breast cancer turned critical, she was moved to the ICU. Her primary nurse denied allowing our kids to visit her, as is ICU policy, although we'd been told by the doctor that the visit would be allowed. I was livid, and I was practically screaming at the nurse. She went to check with the lead doctor of the ICU, and the kids were allowed in for a short visit.

It created an awkward and tense situation, and I felt the nurse was not happy about my outburst. I stepped aside with the nurse and apologized. We had enough stress, and I didn't want issues with the nurse who would be caring for my wife. To my surprise, the nurse smiled and waved off my apology. She told me she would have felt the same way, and she even said she'd hope her husband would do the same in such a situation. It turned out the doctor forgot to inform her of the situation. I may not have really owed her an apology considering the situation, but by being considerate of her and communicating, any awkwardness and tension disappeared, and we had nothing but terrific interactions with her after that.

I've reflected on this many times since that day and have learned that **communication and humility can reap tremendous benefits.** Be gracious to others and communicate openly, and your world will become far more pleasant and productive.

—*Daily inspiration by Patrick P. Long, International Best-Selling Author*

14.

Thought for the Day

"Life shrinks or expands in proportion to one's courage."

—ANAIS NIN

15.

Send Out Ripples of Light and *Shine*!

"Step out of hiding onto the center stage of your life."

—REBECCA HALL GRUYTER

The calling of my heart is to help others know how valuable, gifted, and wonderfully made they are—and that means you! This is because I know, deeply, that you are a light that can shine so brightly that it can be seen even in the darkness. You can be the light of hope and encouragement for another! Whether it's in your business, volunteer work, relationships, or strangers, you can send out rippling rays of light wherever you are.

—**Daily inspiration by Rebecca Hall Gruyter, Influencer and Empowerment Leader**

16.

May Showers

May showers mimicked tears that she cried in the passenger seat as we drove home from the hospital. As her face flushed of all vibrancy, and the look of worry and regret replaced the gleam in her eyes that I worshipped, a piece of me died with it.

When she told me she was sick and that she'd done it to herself, I let my resentment fade and placed my hand upon her knee as she gazed sheepishly through the window at passing trees and passing cars.

In May, I draw inspiration from our own sobrieties. I am grateful my mother decided she'd had enough. I am grateful for the new journey and struggle to become all the things I always knew were possible for us.

I will always reflect on May as the month that changed our lives.

What are you releasing and letting "May showers" wash away, clean, and create space for growth? What are you choosing to plant and create room for growth in your life?

I look forward to seeing all you will plant and grow as we bloom and shine together.

—*Daily inspiration by Leigh Bursey, Musician, Speaker, and Municipal Councillor*

17.

Thought for the Day

"Life is what happens when you're busy making other plans."

—JOHN LENNON

18.

Thought for the Day

"Not how long, but how well you have lived is the main thing."

—SENECA

19.

Thought for the Day

"Don't be afraid of the dark. Shine!"

—VERA NAZARIAN,
THE PERPETUAL CALENDAR OF INSPIRATION

20.

We Need You to *Shine*

"What sets you apart can sometimes feel like a burden, and it's not... A lot of the time, it's what makes you great."

—EMMA STONE

You have special talents, skills, and abilities unique to you. Your special combination of life experience and talent is absolutely needed in the world. No one else can bring your unique combination forward like you.

Stop.

Please read those sentences again and think about that for a moment.

You know things that no one else knows. You see things from a perspective no one else sees. You can do things no one else can do.

As a result, there are specific people you're here to serve. They need your expertise to help them with particular problems they're having. And **they need it in exactly the way you do what you do.**

This is important, *and* **this is your call to step forward.** Now, the big question is, are you willing to help the people you're here to help? It is your choice. I hope you lean in and say yes.

—Daily inspiration by Rebecca Hall Gruyter, Influencer and Empowerment Leader

21.

What Role Are You Celebrating?

"At the end of the day, my most important title is still Mom-in-Chief."

—MICHELLE OBAMA

I am a pediatrician, a wife, a daughter, a sister, a granddaughter, a niece, a cousin, a friend, and a woman. All of these titles are important, and all of these titles I treasure. **But there will never be a title I cherish more than mother.** I could never imagine that two little boys could warm my entire body with the word "mommy." I will hold them tightly whenever they need me. I will guide them throughout their lives the best that I can. Every pain that they feel, I will feel inside me. Each success that they have, my heart will swell. **Being a mother is not all that I am, but it will forever be my greatest accomplishment.**

What title/role are you cherishing and celebrating today?

—*Daily inspiration by Dr. Sarah Breen*

22.

Thought for the Day

"It doesn't matter who you are, where you come from. The ability to triumph begins with you. Always."

—OPRAH WINFREY

23.

Mother's Day Wisdom

"The influence of a mother in the lives of her children is beyond calculation."

—JAMES E. FAUST

As a mother, your actions and your words are guiding your teen's behavior and shaping the attitudes and beliefs that they will carry into adulthood.

What do you react to?

How you respond (or react) to stress and frustration influences how your teen regulates their emotions, especially in times of distress. Handling challenges in a calm and productive manner encourages your teen to problem-solve versus lash out when they feel frustrated or stressed.

Do you "walk your talk"?

Be who you say you want your teen to be because they will notice the hypocrisy between your words and actions. They learn more from your actions than from your words.

What do you do when you make a mistake?

Pivot your mindset from excuses and blame to admitting to making a mistake. Talk openly about how you might avoid making the same mistake in the future.

A mother's kindness and respect will last a lifetime and ripple out to your teen and others.

The stronger your relationship with your teen, the more influence you will have on your teen's values and their long-term choices.

You have a greater impact than you might think (and your teen won't tell you, so I am telling you now).

Happy Mother's Day!

—Daily inspiration by Dr. Kimberly Schehrer, Teen Breakthrough Expert

24.

Thought for the Day

"Never be ashamed of what you feel. You have the right to feel any emotion that you want, and to do what makes you happy. That's my life motto."

—DEMI LOVATO

25.

Thought for the Day

"Don't ever underestimate the impact that you may have on someone else's life."

—ANONYMOUS

26.

Strength Supplied

Oftentimes a person loses their way; their strength wilted and faded away, and seemingly dies. Napoleon Hill, the author and founder of sciences of success, quotes, "Strength and growth come only through continuous effort and struggle." Strength comes from mental toughness, determined to remain focused and to stay on course, regardless of the challenges. **Throughout our life, we will have difficulties and struggles.** Some challenges are so close to the heart and home that we are left feeling like a spinning top, going around and around. How do we get off this unwanted ride? Resilience, courage, determination, and purpose help us get off the ride and stand in our strength and power.

I personally acknowledge I'm only human, I can't do it alone, and I need help. In nature, as I walk or sit in the park, I may cry, sing, and pray to God. In my surrendering moments, I find peace coming into my mind with a sense of guidance and instruction from God. I become renewed and energized, knowing I can and will make it further as my future holds greater possibilities. **These surrendered moments give me courage, build my resilience, and renew my purpose.**

A measure of strength is given to everyone; it is up to you how you will choose to nurture and develop it. Be willing to slow down, seek support, and step forward with courage.

—*Daily inspiration by Toni Stone Bruce, Precious Stones 4 Life, LLC*

27.

Thought for the Day

*"In total darkness it only takes
a little light to shine the way."*

—ARI GUNZBURG, THE LITTLE BOOK OF GREATNESS:
A PARABLE ABOUT UNLOCKING YOUR DESTINY

28.

Believe in *You*

Six months had passed since I held the letter that finalized our divorce. Profound relief and peace washed over me as I paused in my life as a single Mamapreneur to reflect on what it took to set myself free from an unhealthy situation that was draining away my life's energy. I had settled for way less than what I deserved and was paying a high price. I heard myself whisper in the eye of the storm, "**You *deserve more*,**" and everything changed.

The same is true for my financial life. As a single young woman in my 'twenties, I'm sad to say I struggled, living paycheck-to-paycheck with zero planning or net of emergency savings beneath me.

Until I learned about the invisible force that *drives* our financial decisions and behavior without our awareness—our money beliefs (aka, our money mindset). Without realizing it, I believed I had to *struggle* financially because "that's just the way it is." I also believed I was powerless to change this "fact"—a double whammy. So what shifted? **I got clear on my money story and limiting money beliefs—and realized these beliefs were simply not true.** I eventually was able to hear my heart whisper, "*You don't have to suffer anymore; the suffering you've brought upon yourself,*" and everything changed.

The greatest gift that's empowered me to bloom and *shine* is learning this: **We create exactly what we believe.**

—*Daily inspiration by Marlene Elizabeth, author of* Moneywings™

29.

New Normal

The year 2020 began well for most of us. Then we had the pandemic, and we were confined to our homes, so the germs weren't spread.

This caused us to get back to basics and become families again. We spend our days together, creating a new normal.

This brought me back to when my mother spent time with us as kids. We sat out back at night and played instruments and sang with the neighbors. There were other times where we did the same at my grandparents' house. On one occasion, we had about sixty family members gathered and had lots of fun singing and playing many different instruments.

As you take a moment in May to stop and pause, what do you want to purposely build in your new normal? As we go forward, what memory or tradition do you want to build into your life?

When our normal patterns are interrupted, we have an opportunity to build new patterns and habits and make sure they are in line with what matters most to us. This interruption gives us an opportunity to realign with our purpose.

—*Daily inspiration by Catherine M. Laub, Podcast Host*

30.

"Who's Ready to Reach the World?"

Several years ago, I found myself saying *yes* to an opportunity to create an online TV channel with VoiceAmerica. I knew almost nothing about what I was getting into; the project stood in front of me, ready to manifest. In a few days, I was going to host one of my live Women's Empowerment daylong events.

I stood on the stage of the event to give my talk, and something came to me that was so miraculous. Something that I would not have even thought of thinking! It was such a God thing at that moment. It came to me to share the project and announce to the audience, **"So, who will join me? Who's ready to reach the world and be on this journey with me? I don't know where it'll go, but I know it's not just for me. It's for all of you! Who's with me?"**

I paused, wondering what I had just done. To my delight, people stood up and got on that stage! It was an amazing moment of excitement, possibility, and love. Some did sign up that day, as well as others later. We launched it as scheduled, and within just a few months, it became the number-one, most-watched channel.

My lessons are these: **You don't always know how your yes is going to be accomplished. You don't have to do it alone. And it's always about something bigger than yourself. Who can you invite to join you on your journey?**

—*Daily inspiration by Rebecca Hall Gruyter, Influencer and Empowerment Leader*

31.

Your Legacy

*"Intuition is a spiritual facility, and does not
explain, but simply points the way."*

—FLORENCE SCOVEL SHINN

Are you among those folks who routinely have gut feelings, and you follow your instincts?

Or, do you belong to the camp that ignores inklings?

What will the record of your life journey look like?

In the era when I graduated from high school, the college track was not the norm as it is for this generation. Only a few of us had aspirations that required a college degree or specific education: doctor, teacher, and nurse. The rest of us would get a job and get on with the business of life.

Since then, I've come to realize we'd already begun the process of creating our legacy as soon as we drew our first breath. Our legacy isn't the "stuff" we accumulate; it's the *stuff we do* every single minute of every day. How we treat each other, our loved ones, business associates, Mother Earth, and ourselves with respect, compassion, and kindness. Sometimes it may take every ounce of creativity and inspiration to keep our stuff together and have faith that this too shall pass.

My legacy is sharing on-going stories, my own, and encouraging you to share yours because *nobody can tell your story from your perspective except you!*

Grab a notebook and start recording the stuff like wonderful coincidences, incredible insights, and powerful Spirit-filled moments in your life in a journal. You'd be amazed at the legacy you have already created!

—Daily inspiration by Mary E. Knippel, Writer Unleashed

June

1.

Thought for the Day

"Recognise that every interaction you have is an opportunity to make a positive impact on others."

—SHEP HYKEN

2.

You Are Precious

A gem or precious stone is sought after due to its value, beauty, and quality. Because of these components of a gem, it will never be found lying on the street, but rather, in an environment where it must be dug out of rocks and hard ground, deep under the surface of the earth, from where it seems impossible for anything good or of value to come. The long, tiring hours of searching and hard work pay off. The stones that are found will be treated and polished into beautiful and costly jewels.

Did you know you are just like these precious gems? Sometimes your most valued qualities are created in those dark, deep places. Your abilities, skills, and talents many times are deeply rooted and entwined with life's struggles and circumstances. However, that ember glowing with hope, still hot from the fire of circumstances, refuses to smolder out, waiting for that word of encouragement that will polish you so that you can shine in your beauty, gifts, and light.

Like a plant emerging from the soil, like a diamond being polished into greatness, your time has arrived, and your best radiates outward from within. The right opportunities, the perfect conditions, where your abilities, skills, and talents have been developed, and your inner beauty is being sought after. When you share your beauty, gifts, and talents, you shine like the most precious of gems. Be willing to shine.

—*Daily inspiration by Toni Stone Bruce, Precious Stones 4 Life, LLC*

3.

Summer Is a Great Time to *Shine*!

We are halfway through the year, approaching the 3rd Quarter. I toast you with my fresh, minty, lemony iced tea. Here's to you!

And it's the perfect opportunity to take a look at where we are. Are we doing the things that matter most to us? Are we purposefully doing those things that bring us forward? Are we choosing to *shine* and echo out those things into our families, business, community, and world?

Between the delicious summer moments of absorbing sunshine, eating barbeque, taking long walks, sitting with our summer reading books, also take some moments of reflection. Do a "check-in" on **what is important for you to build into your life that nourishes you, is positive, and helps you grow?**

In what ways can you stay mindful of the types of things that get poured into you and to make sure they include practices that will uplift, feed, encourage, and empower you?

This type of insight can come into your consciousness and become part of you, just like your wonderful memories of long summer evenings with loved ones and ice cream with friends on a hot day. Just remember to take time to stop, pause, listen, and choose with purpose.

—*Daily inspiration by Rebecca Hall Gruyter, Influencer and Empowerment Leader*

4.

Summer Fun

Summer is my favorite season by far. The flowers have bloomed, and everything feels calmer. School is out, and it is time to relax. **Even with adult responsibilities, it is important to play.** It is not too hot yet, and nature is beautiful. Smell the flowers. Take the hike. Lay on the hammock. Explore with the kids. Take time to do something fun that brings you peace and joy.

—*Daily inspiration by Dr. Sarah Breen*

5.

Thought for the Day

*"Be a wildflower
amongst cut flowers."*

—DAHI TAMARA KOCH

6.

Celebrating Father Figures

"Children of the new millennium, when change is likely to continue, and stress will be inevitable, are going to need, more than ever, the mentoring of an available father."

—IAN GRANT

Family roles have changed over the years. Dads were thought of as mostly the breadwinners of the family, and mothers were expected to stay home with the kids and run the household. In the new age of the 21st century, mothers may be the breadwinners of the family or at least desire more equality in the household. And fathers may be the stay-at-home parent raising the children and running the household or are actively involved with the family's daily life.

Engaged and present fathers seem to parent a bit differently than mothers, thereby bringing more balance and different benefits to their children. Children raised with fathers who are present are shown to have more empathy, more self-confidence, tend to do better in school, and to avoid more high-risk behaviors. Above all else, they tend to have more healthy and stable relationships when they grow up.

If you are a single mom (or even married) and your children's father isn't involved, what can you do?

Involve your children in an activity where there are positive male role models, such as a Boys Club in your community or a sport with a male coach.

If your children's father is involved, what can you do?

Express gratitude for his role in the family of being a leader, a confidant, a friend, and a hero (thank you, Dad)!

—Daily inspiration by Dr. Kimberly Schehrer, Teen Breakthrough Expert

7.

Victory

"Three feet from gold."

—SHARON LECHTER AND DR. GREG REID

Many in history have stopped just short of victory. Many have the courage to take the first step, the willingness to begin *until* things get tough. Until things get hard. Instead of allowing failure to inspire us, we often let it stop us when victory might be in the very next try. Be willing to try again and push forward. Victory is just around the corner. You can do this!

—Daily inspiration by Dr. Cheryl Lentz, The Academic Entrepreneur

184 | BLOOM & SHINE!

8.

Thought for the Day

*"Remember that the sun always shines
even after stormy days."*

—GIOVANNIE DE SADELEER

9.

Stand Tall

June in Canada is a diverse mix of walking traffic, summer dresses, boats humming across the waterfront, and activism on the steps of our public institutions.

As summer songs of classic rock decorate marinas and the steam begins to rise from the asphalt of our streets, rainbow flags and drag queens march to strengthen their identities. They march to celebrate their individualities, to commemorate their tragedies, and to hold their colorful heads up high.

As we celebrate pride month across a nation that I call home, the pride parades march forward to electrify the streets.

In June, I celebrate my brothers, my sisters, the theys, thems, and us.

What are you standing for and celebrating in your life? What are you proud of this month that you lean into? What can we stand with, on, and for in life?

In June, I stand in solidarity with all colors of the spectrum, shining bright and vivid. Be willing to stand for you. Be willing to celebrate you and those around so we can all *shine*!

—Daily inspiration by Leigh Bursey, Musician, Speaker, and Municipal Councillor

10.

Uniquely Extraordinary

"The only difference between an extraordinary life and an ordinary one is the extraordinary pleasures you find in ordinary things."

—VERONIQUE VIENNE

Are you one of those many women who are artists of the everyday, hiding their gifts because they believe they are ordinary instead of uniquely extraordinary?

When I was diagnosed with breast cancer for the first time, I was grateful to have Stage 0 and dove back into my life as if nothing had happened. Three years later, I received the same diagnosis. This time, I saw it as my wake-up call to not wait any longer to live the life I was destined to lead. To start sharing my writing and speaking up for myself and for all the women who had been silent too long. Perhaps you are not called to write or be a speaker, and only you know what specifically you are called to do.

All your life experiences have brought you to where you are right now. What is important is to shine the light on this moment and how you receive your unexpected gifts, how you cope with them, and, most importantly, what you do next.

Your life-altering experiences provide the opportunity for you to step into owning your story. How do you shine as the hero that you are in your own story? How do you show the world you are a phenomenal hero and not just a supporting player in somebody else's story?

—Daily inspiration by Mary E. Knippel, Writer Unleashed

11.

Thought for the Day

"Every strike brings me closer to the next home run."

–BABE RUTH

12.

Thought for the Day

"You only live once, but if you do it right, once is enough."

—MAE WEST

13.

You Are Needed
Someone Needs What You Have to Offer

No matter how good something is, there are always people out there who don't see the value in it, don't need it, or just don't want it. Don't get deterred when you encounter disinterest or rejection, and don't assume there aren't people out there who do want or need what you have to offer. **Every skill, every talent, and every story has value.**

This is true even for your greatest failures, biggest mistakes, and worst experiences. We learn far more from our mistakes and failures than from successes. We also learn from traumatic and tragic experiences. When I wrote a book about our battle with my wife's cancer and her passing, I shared painful experiences and deeply personal mistakes and feelings I was afraid to share. I nearly didn't share them out of fear but ultimately felt compelled to do so. I have been shocked and amazed to find that the experiences I feared sharing the most have been the most touching and inspirational to others.

When we share what we've learned and what we've experienced, it helps others, and in turn, we benefit from others' stories in a wonderfully reciprocating network of stories and relationships. Empower yourself by sharing your powerful story and experience, and be open and accepting of others. You might just be stunned by what you'll learn and how much you'll grow.

—Daily inspiration by Patrick P. Long, International Best-Selling Author

14.

Thought for the Day

"I've always had a philosophy that position doesn't define power. Impact defines power. What impact are you making on people? What impact are you making on business?"

—MINDY GROSSMAN

15.

Words Are A Gift

The Bible has a verse that goes like this: "Let no unwholesome word proceed from your mouth; but only such a word as is good for edification according to the need of the moment that it may give grace to those who hear."

Growing up, I thought unwholesome words were just a list of the four-letter sort. In reality, unwholesome words can take a lot of forms. Ridicule. Condemnation. Gossip. Complaining.

I've been thinking a lot about that second part of the verse. What if we really did only use words that edified? What if our words gave grace to those who heard them?

What does it even mean to edify? To edify means to build up and cause growth. To strengthen. They don't destroy or tear down.

And what about words that give grace? Grace is basically a gift. Something unmerited by the recipient. Gift words. Wow—what a concept.

Imagine how it would affect the people we interact with day to day if we made it our goal to let our words be a gift—in real life and on social media! Can we pause and consider what we are about to say to see if it really would strengthen, edify, and lift up the hearer?

—Daily inspiration by Shannon McKee, Author, Mentor, and Life Coach

16.

Thought for the Day

"Do what we can, summer will have its flies."
—RALPH WALDO EMERSON

17.

What Does it Mean to "Lean In"?

For me, leaning in means **to step into what it is you are being called to do**. It means staying open to being seen, to serve, and to *shine*. Yes, there will be fears, and there will be challenges, yet you are pulled by your vision to go forward, to touch the lives of others, to share and care in wondrous ways.

Former First Lady Michelle Obama shared this story in her book *Becoming*. When Barack was making the decision to run for president, Michelle felt very uncertain about this step. She had a family, a career, a life she enjoyed with her husband, and she knew all of that would change the moment he announced his candidacy. However, after deep reflection, she realized that this was what they were called to do. So, she leaned in, clearly knowing her *why*, even as she didn't yet know where this journey would take her and her family.

Leaning in means **to show up, perfect in our "imperfections."** If all of the famous leaders and influencers waited until everything was in place, every single mistake they could make was made, their future plans had all of the Ts crossed and Is dotted, I believe they would never have made any change happen at all!

—*Daily inspiration by Rebecca Hall Gruyter, Influencer and Empowerment Leader*

18.

Thought for the Day

"I am in awe of flowers.
Not because of their colors,
but because even though they
have dirt in their roots,
they still grow.
They still bloom."

—D. ANTOINETTE FOY

19.

Thought for the Day

"Genius is in the idea. Impact,
however, comes from action."

—SIMON SINEK

20.

Care for Yourself and Loved Ones

Your success depends on balancing between what you give, what you receive, and your internal disposition to avoid disappointments. Remember that externally you are what you give in thoughts, words, and deeds. Here are simple tools to live powerfully and positively:

Discernment. Your ability to discriminate between people and things that add value to your life and the ones that don't, to recognize those who can genuinely make good use of your offerings and avoid waste.

Align with your values. Attachment is the foundation for hope. You must remain attached to your personal values and principles; they are your identity. These are your non-negotiable life principles. Remember, you are always better off being alone than being in bad company.

Focus on efforts, not the outcomes. You are always in control of your efforts and not the outcomes. Learn how to find satisfaction in your efforts as opposed to the outcomes. Whether or not something turns out good, if you are proud and satisfied with your efforts, then you've given your best. If you did not do your best, don't dwell on it but make a firm resolution to do better next time because life is a journey where history repeats itself.

Appreciate: Appreciate the journey. Celebrate the growth, discovery, and learning.

—Daily inspiration by Fabien W. Edjou, Author & Life Coach

21.

Thought for the Day

"The best way to lengthen out our days is to walk steadily and with a purpose."

—CHARLES DICKENS

22.

What Are You Choosing to Entertain?

Every day, we receive thousands of messages, information, opportunities—some based on positivity and hope, some based on fear and scarcity. With so much input and such busy lives to lead, it can become easy to just allow it all in and move forward the best we can.

Here is what happens: the fear and scarcity creep in slowly and sometimes quietly until you find that you are moving away from your dreams and purpose instead of toward what it is that you want.

It becomes time to draw the line for yourself—what are you choosing to entertain? For me, the inner conversation is to contemplate these questions:

Is this thing meaningful and serving my purpose and my values?

Am I moving forward with ease and positivity?

If any of these answers are no, then I choose to stand my ground and not entertain the opposite of the energy that serves me. *I choose not to hold court for the worry and other negative possibilities.*

Isn't that powerful and purposeful? Yes, it is!

As I'm watching what's happening worldwide and in our country, I am looking for the good, the loving, and the positive that I can entertain. I'm looking for what we can unite around and claim, to bring forward for health and healing and vibrancy and collaboration.

What are the positive things that you can see in the world? *Into what are you choosing to put your energy?*

—*Daily inspiration by Rebecca Hall Gruyter, Influencer and Empowerment Leader*

23.

Thought for the Day

"The question isn't who is going to let me; it's who is going to stop me."

—AYN RAND

24.

Summer "Bless"

What do petunias, daisies, and California poppies all have in common? They all belong to a group of over twelve beautiful summer flowers that actually *thrive* in the heat. If you're winter-born like me and your spirit starts to fizzle as soon as hot weather arrives, prepare a plan to keep blooming and *shining* (like those tough and dainty summer garden flowers).

Here's how to bless yourself this summer (and in any season that raises difficult and/or painful challenges): Treat yourself to an ice-cold glass of strawberry lemonade, sweet peach tea, or fruit-infused water. Crank up the fan or A/C. Take several deep, relaxing breaths as you admire that cheery, bright floral vase of colorful blooms. Kick off your flip-flops. Cozy into your favorite spot (indoors, outdoors, whichever feels right), read your favorite book of sacred writings. As a faith-based entrepreneur, I lean on the Bible for financial wisdom and much more. I encourage you to choose the best spiritual or inspirational text that serves you according to your own faith tradition, religious practices, and/or spiritual beliefs. (Please feel free to reach out for private support for your journey, especially regarding your relationship with money from a spiritual point of view.)

(Bonus gardening tip: Curious about more summer flowers to create the prettiest garden ever? Try hydrangeas, sunflowers, dahlias, daisies, irises, lavender, peonies, and zinnias.)

Enjoy your summer fun in the sun! Be blessed as you bloom and *shine*! :)

—*Daily inspiration by Marlene Elizabeth, author of* Moneywings™

25.

Thought for the Day

"Every great dream begins with a dreamer. Always remember, you have within you the strength, the patience, and the passion to reach for the stars to change the world."

—HARRIET TUBMAN

26.

Success and Happiness

Get out of your own way.

You are the only thing standing in your way to success and happiness. What you choose to believe becomes your truth. How can you shift in thoughts and actions to get out of your own way to move closer toward your goals?

—*Daily inspiration* by **Maureen Ryan Blake, Founder and Principal of** *The Power of the Tribe*

27.

Thought for the Day

"It took me quite a long time to develop a voice and now that I have it, I am not going to be silent."

—MADELEINE ALBRIGHT

28.

Connect to Others from a Place of Service

When you meet someone, and you are thinking about what you can get from them, it shows in the way you talk to them. You can cover it with the logic of how they would benefit, but your true intention always shows through, and the result is that the other person doesn't feel seen, heard, or understood.

So, make sure you **cultivate the spirit of service within yourself** first.

It's perfectly fine to want something for yourself as well, but make sure you are showing up thinking *win-win*. The best way to do this is to see the world through the eyes of the person with whom you're trying to connect. Here is an exercise you can do to prepare yourself for a connection with an individual.

Sit down with a sheet of paper or screen and write out the answers to these questions from their perspective:

What are they most excited about?

What are they looking for?

What are their biggest concerns or frustrations?

What solutions are they seeking?

With this understanding, your ability to connect with them skyrockets. These are also great questions to think about before presenting to an audience. They are also great questions to explore and ask at networking events to facilitate connecting conversations coming from a place of service.

—Daily inspiration by Rebecca Hall Gruyter, Influencer and Empowerment Leader

29.

Thought for the Day

"Stop wearing your wishbone where
your backbone ought to be."

—ELIZABETH GILBERT

206 | BLOOM & SHINE!

30.

Beauty

"If you look for perfection, you will never be satisfied."
—LEO TOLSTOY

"Do not underestimate yourself by comparing yourself to others. It's our differences that make us unique and beautiful."
—RISHIKA JAIN

You know that voice in your head that is constantly criticizing everything you are and everything you do? Yes, that one. That voice in your head telling you that you'd be perfect if you were more or less of something is lying. There's a big difference between being perfect and radiating beauty.

Striving for perfection robs you of your joy. If all your energy is focused on how you are not enough, there is no energy for creating. Have you ever felt good when you've compared yourself to others and wanted to be more like them? The more we strive for perfection, the more miserable we become. **Stop the comparisons. Your inner essence is your beauty.**

It's okay to look at others, see what they are up to, and think, *I'd love to have an experience like that.* It doesn't serve you to envy what others have. Envy and radiating beauty feel different. Envy feels darker and like a dead weight, while beauty feels effervescent and light. One creates a downward spiral stemming from a sense of scarcity. The other puts you on the vibrational path of creating what you desire and uplifts you. **You radiating your inner essence is the most beautiful light in the world.**

—Daily inspiration by Kimi Avary, MA, Relationship Navigation Specialist

July

1.

Are You Nourishing Yourself?

Think for a moment about how you are pouring yourself into others—your clients, team members, family, friends, community. Celebrate how wonderful that is!

And then, think about these questions: **Are you letting other things be the priorities versus letting yourself to be poured into? Are you saying yes to things that feel draining rather than nourishing?**

It's so easy to let ourselves fill our days, say we're "too busy," but keep doing those things and adding more while never checking off all the items on our to-do list.

We love serving others, love to say "yes," and we risk losing ourselves in the process. We are so good at continuing to add things to our plates that we occasionally need to **stop. Pause. Evaluate.** This halfway point in the year is a perfect time to do just that:

Take just one minute to write down all the things that are on your plate right now—the things you're doing, you're committed to doing and getting ready for.

Read the list, noticing what feels pressured and what doesn't. Notice where you're being pulled and where you "need to"

—or should, or have to) take care of things.

Take a good look at the list. You want to make sure that you are making choices that are on *purpose* for you. Remember, you can choose to say no and take things off this list.

Do you still choose all that is on your list?

—Daily inspiration by Rebecca Hall Gruyter, Influencer and Empowerment Leader

2.

Thought for the Day

"Shine your light and make a positive impact on the world; there is nothing so honorable as helping improve the lives of others."

—ROY T. BENNETT

3.

Thought for the Day

"What you do has far greater impact than what you say."

– STEPHEN COVEY, AUTHOR AND EDUCATOR

4.

Lead from Generosity

I have found leading from a place of generosity has simplified my life. When faced with a decision, simply chose to be generous with your time, compassion, love, and faith. Everything then becomes clear. Choose to give, lead, and love richly and generously.

—*Daily inspiration* by **Maureen Ryan Blake, Founder and Principal of** *The Power of the Tribe*

5.

Thought for the Day

"I've learned that people will forget what you said, people will forget what you did, but people will never forget how you made them feel."

—MAYA ANGELOU

6.

Good Timing

Good Timing Isn't an Accident.

Good timing is rarely a matter of luck or fortune, even though it may feel as if it is and also may appear so to outside observers. **However, you make good timing happen through your persistent efforts. Don't wait for the right time, but rather, pursue the right time.**

It is often said that success is a matter of being in the right place at the right time. The way to be in the right place at the right time is to keep putting yourself in the right places. The timing may be wrong repeatedly, and then finally, it will all come together. Go after your dream persistently until the right time intersects your continued efforts. No one ever succeeds by sitting at home on the couch watching TV. Be patient, be persistent, and stay involved. Participate in activities, get your information in front of people, network, and get ready for success!

"Patience is the calm acceptance that things can happen in a different order than the one you have in mind."

—DAVID G. ALLEN

—Daily inspiration by Patrick P. Long, International Best-Selling Author

7.

Thought for the Day

"One of the most courageous things you can do is identify yourself, know who you are, what you believe in and where you want to go."

–SHEILA MURRAY BETHEL

8.

July Reflections

For me, July recalls the joyous sounds of group singalongs—lyrics sung in unison by masses of the melting pot. The feeling of frantic energy runs through my veins as the audience sways and jumps and erupts to the chorus of our favorite songs.

As a musician, our band performances are a special opportunity to connect with the spirits of others through the beat of the music.

July is everything that I wait for every year. I am inspired by music, kinship, and anonymity as I celebrate the soundtrack of life.

What does July bring to your mind? What special summer moments do you celebrate? What special moments of connection are creating the soundtrack of your life? What is your special tune?

Music can touch our hearts and bring us together powerfully without a word being said. Today, share a musical moment with another.

—*Daily inspiration by Leigh Bursey, Musician, Speaker, and Municipal Councillor*

9.

Showing Up

My sister is a runner. Some time ago, she ran a double marathon. Yes, that's 52.4 miles. And it was on trails in a national park. With lots of hills. And mud. It was a life goal and a test of endurance for this mom of four to push herself like that. I, on the other hand, did nothing for this race. I didn't pay her fee. I didn't train with her. I didn't fill out her registration or prepare her drop bags, or pick up her race packet. Nothing.

And, yet, when it was finished, and we were all done crying, she thanked me. **She** thanked *me*. Why? Because I showed up. That's it. I just showed up to cheer her on throughout the day. My presence meant something. That I would drag my sorry butt out of bed at three o'clock in the morning and be there when she needed a familiar face.

That's true in life too, you know. Sometimes the power of just being there for another is the critical thing. The fact that you didn't leave when the going got tough in your marriage. Or that you came home for dinner when you could have worked another hour. Or that you sat down to listen to your daughter's favorite song even though you really don't like hip-hop music.

We think we need to buy something or say something profound. But often, we just need to show up. How can you show up for another in your life today?

—*Daily inspiration by Shannon McKee, Author, Mentor, and Life Coach*

10.

Are You an Empath?

For many years, my mental illnesses were controlled with medication, so it didn't cause any challenges. Unfortunately, as time went on, the medications lost their effect. It wasn't until after my husband, Tony, died that I realized the problems stemmed from me being an *empath*. This means I absorb others' negative energies. Between April 2019 and February 2020, I was in dismay. My mother died, then Tony got ill. He ultimately died on February 25, 2020.

Tony was depressed and stressed. His stress, my stress, the family's stress created a lot of difficult and challenging energy to be around and absorb. It never dawned on me to protect myself in my own home.

As an *empath*, it is important to protect yourself in any way possible. You can simply ask for Jesus' precious light to surround you. Another way is by imagining roots growing from your feet and planted to the core of Mother Earth. Find what is right for you.

Especially during these challenging times, empaths can pick up and absorb energy and feelings that are not truly yours. It is important to build a practice of checking in to protect your energy, emotions, and feelings so that you are not picking up what is not yours to carry.

I encourage you to tap into your own feelings and begin to watch when you are with others if your energy shifts. If it does, you may be an *empath*.

—*Daily inspiration by Catherine M. Laub, Podcast Host*

11.

Thought for the Day

"Do not dwell in the past, do not dream of the future, concentrate the mind on the present moment."

—BUDDHA

12.

Thought for the Day

"The only person you are destined to become is the person you decide to be."

—RALPH WALDO EMERSON

13.

Thought for the Day

"A friend is a gift you give yourself."
—ROBERT LOUIS STEVENSON

14.

Path to Greatness

At various times throughout our entire life, we all have that someone that impacted our lives by something that was expressed or some action taken that made such a significant difference that we clung to the memory. We follow. It's important to realize we need to start to create our own path, to follow the way we're made to shine. We realize, at some point in time, *I have followed you through this winding road, and now I must choose.* Do we allow fear to choose the road with which we are familiar? Or do we decide to take a path of faith, hope, and forgiveness, three essentials to greatness?

This path brings joy, peace, and a fulfilled life. It allows you to become who you were destined to be and created to be with a divine purpose within. Greatness can be loyalty, keeping one's word, and seeing the best in others. Which path will you choose? I hope you lean in and choose your own beautiful path back to greatness.

—Daily inspiration by Toni Stone Bruce, Precious Stones 4 Life, LLC

15.

Thought for the Day

*"If life were predictable it would cease
to be life, and be without flavor."*

—ELEANOR ROOSEVELT

16.

Core Values

"Love is an expression and assertion of self-esteem, a response to one's own values in the person of another."

—AYN RAND, ATLAS SHRUGGED

"You complete me," Jerry said passionately to Dorothy in the movie, *Jerry McGuire*. While it may seem romantic, I would have preferred to hear him tell her that she was inspired by her to be his best self. When you are dependent on someone else to complete us, it means you feel, on some level, inadequate on your own.

Instead of looking for someone to complete you, look to be the best version of yourself. Polish your edges so you can shine your radiance. Look for someone who compliments your core values. If you're unsure what your core values are, pause and imagine being the Fairy Godmother to everyone in the world. What do you want for them? Love? Dignity? Happiness? Abundance? Integrity? Connection? Joy? Peace? Integrity? What are those things without which your life would be meaningless or unfulfilling? Those are your core values.

Write them down and live by them. Make your core values the root of everything you are and everything you do. They are the foundation upon which you build your life. The world around you mirrors what is happening inside of you. The depth of your core values within yourselves is a mirror for what you are attracting in your life.

—Daily inspiration by Kimi Avary, MA, Relationship Navigation Specialist

17.

Thought for the Day

"To love beauty is to see light."
—VICTOR HUGO

18.

Happy Independence Month to Your Teen!

*"Together, may we give our children the
roots to grow and the wings to fly."*

—AUTHOR UNKNOWN

Many parents think of independence as having the life skills to live successfully, the maturity to make reasonable choices, and the practice of staying safe and healthy.

Many teens define independence as having the freedom to make decisions both wise and foolish, define their own rules at the game of life, depend on their parents less and less, and have fun, fun, fun!

Could both define independence? I believe so!

However, giving your teen greater independence by their definition can be terrifying! Many parents attempt to keep their teens safe by controlling their life, planning their days, and taking care of their problems *for* them. This disempowers your teen and does not guide them to greater independence.

Tips for parents to guide their teen to more independence:

1. Give your teen practice in gaining work skills: managing household tasks, filling out a job application, or preparing for a job or school interview.

2. Teach financial skills: creating a budget, investing, credit cards, and debt. Have them create a sample budget and shop for groceries one week out of the month to get a real sense of a typical household expense.

3. Have them practice goal setting and breaking down the steps to achieve that goal. Encourage them to enjoy the journey, not just the end-result, and to celebrate each step achieved no matter how small!

—Daily inspiration by Dr. Kimberly Schehrer, Teen Breakthrough Expert

19.

Thought for the Day

*"Every action we take impacts the
lives of others around us."*

—ARTHUR CARMAZZI

20.

Just As You Are

What can hold us back from being *blooming* and *shining* can be our own assumptions about the value of our qualities. We can ask ourselves: *What do I possibly have to contribute? I'm too shy to be a speaker. For people to respect me, I have to be [shorter, taller, thinner, heavier, better dressed, more eloquent]!*

Have you ever had statements like these looping in your brain?

For a long time, I hid my laugh because I was told it wasn't professional, so I *assumed* that it was a terrible quality for a serious businesswoman/ speaker/leader. Then a coach told me that it was part of who I am and to embrace it. I felt empowered to lean in, even to this part of me, and what did I find? People leaned into me even closer and laughed with me! In fact, that was what they remembered and loved about me, and it always made them smile.

Be willing to be seen and heard, to be visible—just as you are.

Sometimes the journey to being visible can be uncomfortable and make you feel vulnerable. But think about this: What if by doing that uncomfortable, difficult, scary thing, you made a difference for another person? Or maybe hundreds or thousands of people? That is your potential power of showing up and leaning in. Share your gifts, your uniqueness, your "you-ness."

—Daily inspiration by Rebecca Hall Gruyter, Influencer and Empowerment Leader

21.

Thought for the Day

"Continuous effort -- not strength nor intelligence -- is the key to unlocking our potential."

—WINSTON CHURCHILL

22.

Reveal Your New Self

All the preparations are now done; it is time to reveal your new and ideal self to the world. Jubilant as any fresh plant, be proud to let the world see your new and ideal self. Observe nature and notice that plants strive to grow as tall and as high as possible toward the light. You, too, are on a path to growth toward luminous heights. You should strive to grow as long as there is a living breath in your body.

Strive to spread as wide as possible. Don't dim your light just to please others or simply because it bothers others. Just like you, they too have the same right to grow as tall and wide as possible. The time has come to put it all together. You know who you are, you understand your environment, you know to discern between the external things that add value to your life and the ones that don't. **Putting it all together means orienting your desires only toward your goal and starting to be your ideal self in the way you think, talk, and act so that everything reflects the person you aspire to become.** The vibrancy of July should illuminate your adventurous new path so that you can enjoy every moment's treasures and learn how to have fun with the process.

—*Daily inspiration by Fabien W. Edjou, Author & Life Coach*

23.

Thought for the Day

"We are all faced with a series of great opportunities brilliantly disguised as impossible situations."

–CHUCK SWINDOLL,
CHRISTIAN PASTOR AND RADIO PREACHER

24.

Freedom to Bloom

As we celebrate the blessings of freedom, these song lyrics often tap in my mind:

"Freedom is sometimes just simply another perspective away...who could you be if your lens was changed for a moment... would you still be the same?"

—"PERSPECTIVES" BY KUTLESS

I invite you to take time for yourself to pause and reflect on the following statement as it applies to your life:

I am free to experience the love and life I deserve.

If you agree (cue the fireworks; fire the cannons of confetti), congratulations! May the wind always be at your back and may you go from strength to strength. Your attitude empowers others to believe and do the same.

If you're finding this statement does not easily ring true for you, take time to journal your reason(s) why. Notice any belief(s) you hold that may conflict with this statement. What if you could gently set aside that belief for just a moment (you can put it right back anytime)? Would the statement now be true for you?

This exercise may require several sittings throughout the month (or year). It takes courage to challenge our beliefs. Remember to take deep breaths as you consider your beliefs. Enjoy nibbles of dark chocolate, a favorite beverage, a cozy blanket, or a sunny park bench. Exploring our beliefs definitely calls for big doses of compassion and self-care.

—*Daily inspiration by Marlene Elizabeth, author of Moneywings™*

25.

Impossible?

"It is only impossible until someone does it."

This quote always fascinates me because of so many naysayers who say that it cannot be done—regardless of what it is. Instead of getting mad at those who doubt you, your belief, and the outcome, prove them wrong. Success is truly the best revenge. Thank them for the motivation, smile sweetly, and then show them that you did it—no need to argue, as the results will speak for themselves. Having faith in yourself, particularly when you know you know, is often the hardest part of the success equation. Never give up and never give in to the fear. When doubt comes (and it will), simply smile to yourself knowing that someday, one day, you will prove them all wrong. Show them it is possible! Ah, what a day that will be!

—*Daily inspiration by Dr. Cheryl Lentz, The Academic Entrepreneur*

26.

Thought for the Day

"The whole secret of a successful life is to find out what is one's destiny to do, and then do it."

—HENRY FORD

27.

Thought for the Day

"Life is not measured by the number of breaths we take, but by the moments that take our breath away."

—MAYA ANGELOU

28.

Why Visibility Is Important

"If they cannot see you, if then they cannot hear you, then you cannot help them."

—REBECCA HALL GRUYTER

Visibility is about being seen so that we can shine our light to help others along their path. Let's be easy to find.

I was once *very* resistant to being seen—staying invisible was part of my DNA on a cellular level; it was so programmed into me. When I had to be in front of people, I would shake, turn purple, lose my words, and barely be able to say my name! So it was a really long journey to be able to come through that to live and serve in the way that I do today.

I learned that any of the discomforts I might be experiencing was so worth it. If I could make a difference for one other person, to somehow make the path a little bit easier for someone else, then I was willing to be uncomfortable, to stretch outside of my comfort zone, to be vulnerable and imperfect.

To this day, that is still what pulls me forward. I believe that if we tap into our why—to know our purpose, our passion, what we are called to do—it will pull us forward to stretch and succeed on a higher level and *shine* our unique light on the world! What is your why? Will you choose to **shine**?

—Daily inspiration by Rebecca Hall Gruyter, Influencer and Empowerment Leader

29.

Independence

"Whatever your passion is, keep doing it. Don't waste chasing after success or comparing yourself to others. Every flower blooms at a different pace."

—SUZY KASSEM

Independence: ability to act freely, self-confidence, spunk, outspoken, or boldness.

Do any of those descriptions ring a bell for you? No?

Your day of reckoning doesn't have to come with a revolution. It can quietly take a stand for yourself today by turning right instead of left on your evening walk or choose sherbet instead of vanilla.

You don't have to wait until you have a health crisis to put yourself on that to-do list.

Take a bubble bath tonight, schedule a massage before you desperately need it, and claim the freedom to take care of yourself.

Taking care of yourself doesn't mean you'll stop taking care of your loved ones; it means you are choosing to include yourself among those whom you nurture, love, and support.

What did you dream about when you were a kid?

I wanted to be a writer. I wasn't encouraged because it wasn't realistic. However, I never gave up my dream and have been a journalist for over thirty-five years, happily sharing my story and helping many, many other women share theirs.

Start today to rewrite your story and declare your personal Independence Day!

—*Daily inspiration by Mary E. Knippel, Writer Unleashed*

30.

Celebrate Your Freedom

"One flag, one land, one heart, one hand, one nation evermore."
—OLIVER WENDELL HOLMES

It is time to celebrate! Celebrate your freedom. Celebrate the ability to live your life the way you want to live it. Celebrate the fact that you can continue to change your life. As the barbeques end and the fireworks sparkle in the night sky, celebrate the little things as well as the big. What are you choosing to celebrate today?

—Daily inspiration by Dr. Sarah Breen

31.

Thought for the Day

"You must be the change you wish to see in the world."

—GANDHI

August

1.

Thought for the Day

"No matter what you look like or think you look like you're special and loved and perfect just the way you are."

—ARIEL WINTER

2.

Take a Stand for Moving Forward

I've been seeing people bump up against their boundaries during tumultuous times, buffeted back and forth by worry, fear, and constant news of disaster and scarcity. They give in to the negativity they feel all around them and shrink back in their businesses and lives.

Their boundaries around their values, ambitions, and goals become blurred by other people's messages of fear about the future.

When we put our energy into those fears, more fear is created. We then keep on attracting the same, and we continue to shrink and contract instead of expanding, creating new opportunities, and sharing ourselves out into the world. We make small decisions, afraid to struggle and to take risks that will support us in following our dreams once the stormy clouds have parted.

It lights a fire in my belly, a passion that has me stand up and shout, "No! I am not willing to entertain negativity and fear! I am holding strong to my boundaries, taking a stand for *moving forward*." I know that it's hard, but I believe that we cannot allow difficult times to have us shrink back. We are in this together, and **the world needs us most when the challenges are greatest.**

When I see colleagues and clients allow fear to cause them to drop new projects, slash prices, pause their future plans and strategies, what I truly see is that they are dimming their bright light to shine the path for others.

Choose hope and truth instead of fear and move forward!

—Daily inspiration by Rebecca Hall Gruyter, Influencer and Empowerment Leader

3.

Thought for the Day

"You have brains in your head. You have feet in your shoes. You can steer yourself any direction you choose."

—DR. SEUSS

4.

Stand Firm

August brings a prelude of change in seasons and energy. This is the heart of summer and the time for your affirmation. Life is full of energy; the colors in nature are vibrant and lush. This is the time to let the world see and have a taste of the new you. Just as vegetation is lush, so should you act with grace and in abundance. There should be a clear distinction between the old and the new you.

Some may admire the new you while others will dislike it. This is the most accurate way for you to know that you are no longer the person that you used to be. The easiest thing to do is to fall back into old habits just for peace or to please others, but you must not forget that your own identity is at stake. **Regressing will only satisfy your detractors and disappoint the people who admire the new you. There is more to lose by giving up than moving forward. This is the time where you must reaffirm your core principles.**

Everything around you is full of movement that brings all sorts of temptations and possibilities. **You must sink the roots of your conviction as deep as humanly possible.** Stand firm, stand tall. Remember your why and know I am cheering you on! You can do it.

—*Daily inspiration by Fabien W. Edjou, Author & Life Coach*

5.

Thought for the Day

"Be faithful in small things because it is in them that your strength lies."

—MOTHER TERESA

6.

Thought for the Day

"Winter is an etching, spring a watercolor, summer an oil painting and autumn a mosaic of them all."

—STANLEY HOROWITZ

7.

The Meaning of a Song

On August 22, 1998, Tony and I were married, and it truly was the best day of my life!

We chose two wedding songs. One of them was: "Masterpiece" by Atlantic Starr, which has the following two lines in it:

"I've found a **masterpiece** in you

A work of art it's true

This **fairy tale** we shared

Is real inside our hearts."

Tony was my knight in shining armor and did do all he could for me. This is why he was my *masterpiece*!

On May 3, 2020, due to the pandemic, we did a drive-by birthday for my granddaughter, Natalee, age three. This was my first occasion alone since Tony died in February. I was sad and missing him. While waiting in my car, a hotrod approached. He was blasting "Masterpiece," which made me cry. Tony was by my side!

This August would have been our twenty-second anniversary, and we were together twenty-eight years. Tony continues to communicate through songs confirming his love for me.

Do you know someone who may try to communicate with you? If you suddenly hear a familiar song and it relates to someone, they may be reaching out to you. What is the message or reminder for you?

—*Daily inspiration by Catherine M. Laub, Podcast Host*

8.

I Hope You Dance

I greatly admire women wired with left-brain "smarts."

—Where was I when that "super-hero" card was stamped?!) I marvel at their leadership & and master-coordinator magic. My dear reader, you know who you are! You easily manage time (with or without a watch), effortlessly organize *anything* out of order, beautifully calculate numbers to the penny, joyfully edit with speed and accuracy, heroically track and analyze data as if with one arm tied behind your back (I'd go blind!), successfully follow through with even the tiniest project detail, and the most amazing miracle of all—remain patiently cool, calm, and collected under insanely stressful conditions while still being able to *think* clearly, make sound decisions, and lead! A woman who knows her amazing gifts is empowered to *truly* bloom and *shine!*

Sadly, for so long, I suffered the high cost of deeply discounting my own precious *right*-brain contributions. It's taken a lifetime for me to allow my essential gifts to bloom and *shine*. It took me longer to wrap my brain around the fact that I *am* powerful—not *powerless*—and perfect just as I am. So are you! The sweetest joy will be your reward when you let your strengths bloom and *shine*. Remember: doing so is a dance, not a final destination.

"When you get the choice, to sit it out or dance, I hope you dance"

—LEE ANN WOMACK, "I HOPE YOU DANCE"

—Daily inspiration by Marlene Elizabeth, author of Moneywings™

9.

Thought for the Day

"The only limit to your impact is your imagination and commitment."

—TONY ROBBINS

10.

What's Your Mission?

My mission—the calling of my heart—is to help others know how valuable, gifted, and wonderfully made they truly are. I think I knew this even as a little girl, and I followed different paths along the way to find where and how I was meant to shine. I even resisted it sometimes. When I heard God's soft voice in my ear, I would say, "No, not now, not yet!" Me, get up in front of people and speak when I can barely say my name out loud when someone asks? What, share my story in front of hundreds of people? Change my career and leap into something completely different, on my own?

Not now, not yet—or ever!

Yet, here I am today, shining my light and fulfilling my mission to serve in the best way that I'm able. Happier than I have ever been.

When we step forward and share the gift of us, we shine our light out into the world, rippling out rays of light wherever we go. Whether it's on our business, volunteer work, relationships with friends and family, or a stranger on the street, you can be on a mission and share the gift of you with the world.

What is your mission? Where do you shine?

—Daily inspiration by Rebecca Hall Gruyter, Influencer and Empowerment Leader

11.

Thought for the Day

"The unexamined life is not worth living."

—SOCRATES

12.

Prepare for Success in the Coming School Year

"Let us remember: One book, one pen, one child, and one teacher can change the world."

—MALALA YOUSAFZAI

"Back to school" is an exciting time of new classes, new friendships, new school supplies, and cool school clothes. What it really means is *a new beginning*—a blank slate on which your teen is writing the future of that healthy, loving, empowered adult they are to become.

What are some strategies to enhance success?

Set boundaries concerning television, video games, and cell phones. When planned ahead, your teen is more likely to stick to them.

Encourage your teen to set goals. Does your teen want to try out for a sports team or rock science class? Have them write their goals down on paper or digitally so they can track their progress.

Get school supplies that work for them. Color-coded notebooks and folders for each subject help with memory and organization. A digital planner is great for color-coding their calendar, such as family activities, extracurricular activities, exams, and assignments. You can color-code on the family calendar, too.

Your teen may not express it, but they are looking to you to teach them how to succeed in school and in life!

—Daily inspiration by Dr. Kimberly Schehrer, Teen Breakthrough Expert

13.

Thought for the Day

"Remember who you are. Don't compromise for anyone, for any reason. You are a child of the Almighty God. Live that truth."

—LYSA TERKEURST

14.

Showing Up to Make a Difference

Sometimes the journey to blooming and shining can be uncomfortable and make you feel vulnerable. It can feel easier to say *no* and stay safe than to say *yes* and step up. But consider this: What if by doing that uncomfortable, difficult, scary thing, you made a difference for another person? *Or maybe hundreds or thousands of people?*

That is your potential power of showing up and being willing to be seen, to *shine!* What does it take to be willing? Simply:

Show up. Say *yes* to those opportunities that pull at your heart. (Don't worry about how to do it; the *how* will almost always come after the commitment of *yes*.)

Let people support you and cheer you on.

Share what is on your heart.

Reach out your hand and make a difference for one person.

What happens when you take this exciting, uncomfortable, scary, joyful journey? People will say, "Thank you. Thank you for shining a light on my path. Thank you for caring enough, loving enough, being enough to reach out your hand to me, for making a difference in my life." That is how we make a global difference, heart to heart, life to life. How can you show up today and reach your hand out to help another?

—Daily inspiration by Rebecca Hall Gruyter, Influencer and Empowerment Leader

15.

Time Is Precious

We all are given a twenty-four-hour day with equal time to do and accomplish life's responsibilities, desires, and goals.

George Herbert, an English poet, wrote, **"Do not wait, the time will never be just right. Start where you stand, and work with whatever tools you may have at your command, and better tools will be found as you go along."** I believe it is important to make the most of one's time.

This can apply to anything in life that's important to you. The more time you spend using your abilities, the more success and passion will be created. If more time was applied to your family, using your abilities and skills to make life more enjoyable and memorable, the home would be a place where there would be such fond memory and a bonding love. **How are you choosing to spend your time?** Is it on things that matter to you? While you can build a solid foundation at home with an abundance of respect, love, and kindness.

Take time to empower someone, build character, and develop strength. Make time to bring forward the things that are important to you. Be mindful of how you are choosing to spend your time. Time is precious and can be used as a blessing for yourself and others. Spend it wisely.

—Daily inspiration by Toni Stone Bruce, Precious Stones 4 Life, LLC

16.

Art

In recent months I have been amazed at some of the things people create—just normal people who live regular lives. Perhaps even in jobs that are simply paying the bills. Not glamorous, artsy jobs. Just regular work-a-day jobs. But, in the margins, they create. They quilt or needle-point or sing or draw or knit or write or remodel or take photos or sew or papercraft. And their creations share beauty. They show us that there is something beautiful and artistic that is hardwired into all of us. Some creative and original thread that runs deep in our souls.

Edith Schaeffer once said, "Whatever form art takes, it gives outward expression to what otherwise would remain locked in the mind, unshared... Art in various forms expresses and gives opportunity to others to share in, and respond to, things which would otherwise remain vague, empty yearnings. [It] satisfies and fulfills something in the person creating and in those responding."

You've felt that before, haven't you? When you look at a beautiful piece of jewelry or listen to a line of music? Something in you resonates, doesn't it? **I think it strikes such a deep chord because you were created in the image of the Master Artist. One who sculpted the mountains and set the stars in the sky. Because He delights in creating, so do you.**

How are you giving space in your life to create? How can you celebrate creative expression this week?

—*Daily inspiration by Shannon McKee, Author, Mentor, and Life Coach*

17.

Thought for the Day

"Don't be afraid of the dark. Shine!"

—VERA NAZARIAN,
THE PERPETUAL CALENDAR OF INSPIRATION

18.

Be Mindful of What You Feed Yourself

They say you are what you eat, meaning that all of the food you take in can either make your body sicker *or* keep you healthy and fit on a cellular level.

The same is true for what you take in through your mind and spirit. It's important to be mindful of the types of things you let pour into you—the things that you watch, what you listen to, that you're choosing to include. **They become part of your emotional and mental health, part of your very DNA.**

Stop, pause, and look at where you are doing the things that matter most to you. Make sure the things you are doing are truly in alignment with what matters most to you to bring forth. Ask *how you are nourishing yourself in ways that keep you in alignment.*

Make it a practice to be aware of what you are taking in and receiving. Invite into your life the things that feed into you—positive media, messaging that will uplift, encourage, and empower you.

Like choosing healthy food for your body, choose positive, informative, responsible messages that nourish you, uplift you, and help you grow. You're worth it. Be willing to nourish yourself.

—Daily inspiration by Rebecca Hall Gruyter, Influencer and Empowerment Leader

19.

Thought for the Day

"In the middle of difficulty lies opportunity."

—ALBERT EINSTEIN

20.

Small Acts Become Big Reminders

When my wife was diagnosed with breast cancer, our family, friends, and community supported us in myriad ways. Throughout over three years of battling her cancer and beyond her passing, the support continued. I was surprised by some of the creative ways people had of supporting us. Someone landscaped our lawn while we were out one day. It was done anonymously, and I've never learned who did it. One of the things they did was put in a small brick border around a group of bushes in front of our house. To this day, I look at that border every time I walk into the house, and it reminds me of the kindness and generosity of the community surrounding us. It not only reminds me of that particular act, but it also makes me reflect on all the support we received, including gift cards, meals, snacks, toys for our kids, and much more.

Kindness does not result merely in fleeting feelings. Kindness provides a powerful structure in our lives that builds upon itself, providing a foundation that we can continue to build upon.

"Do your little bit of good where you are; it's those little bits of good put together that overwhelm the world."

—DESMOND TUTU

—Daily inspiration by Patrick P. Long, International Best-Selling Author

21.

Thought for the Day

"A leader is a dealer in hope."
—NAPOLEON BONAPARTE, FRENCH
MILITARY LEADER AND EMPEROR

22.

Inner Peace, Contentment

*"Everything has its wonders, even darkness and silence, and
I learn, whatever state I'm in, therein to be content."*

—HELEN KELLER

Inner peace is the ability to find contentment in whatever situation arises in your life.

A monk once told a man who said he had no time to meditate for fifteen minutes a day because his life was too busy that he should meditate daily for an hour. Our busy lives can be full of ups and downs. We label the situations we find ourselves in as good or bad. We welcome some and not others. How you handle the surprises and challenges life offers you will determine how the situation affects you. Are you someone who flows with whatever is happening, or do you find yourself getting stressed?

Did you know that peace is attainable no matter what life serves you? Meditation is a useful tool that you can use regardless of what is happening in your life to find peace. It is spiritual rather than religious, and people of many faiths use it. Spend time every day, quieting your mind in meditation. It grounds you. It helps you strengthen your ability to handle whatever arises. It gives you the ability to observe your life and gain insights. It gives you a vantage point to look for the hidden gems in every situation. The quiet that meditation brings opens space inside you to listen to your inner wisdom. **Challenge yourself and look beyond the circumstances to find your inner wisdom and peace.**

—*Daily inspiration by Kimi Avary, MA, Relationship Navigation Specialist*

23.

Stop. Pause. Listen. Then Choose.

I believe the ability to live on purpose and with purpose is tied closely to stopping, pausing, and listening. June is the perfect month to pause, sit in your garden or yard or a field with a nice cold beverage, shoes kicked off, and legs outstretched. Ah!

Feel the breeze, smell the flowers, and listen to the buzz of the flies, tree frogs, and locusts. And listen within. Living a life on purpose and with purpose means listening for the wisdom your heart has to tell you. Take a deep breath and lean in a little more to the reminder of who you are and what you are called to bring forth.

Then choose your next steps on purpose and in alignment with what matters most to you to bring forward, one breath, step, and choice at a time.

—Daily inspiration by Rebecca Hall Gruyter, Influencer and Empowerment Leader

24.

Stay in Your Step

As an entrepreneur, I can get distracted by "shiny objects" or opportunities that come along while I'm on my path. I find this happens in all of our lives, and is sometimes why we get overwhelmed as we are trying to move too many things forward at once. "Stay in your step" is simply a reminder to finish what you are doing before moving forward. This way, we simplify and take one step at a time. How can you stay in your step today?

—*Daily inspiration by Maureen Ryan Blake, Founder and Principal of The Power of the Tribe*

25.

Thought for the Day

*"You can never have an impact on society
if you have not changed yourself."*

—NELSON MANDELA

26.

Your Own Brilliance

"It's never too late to be what you might have been."
—GEORGE ELIOT, PEN NAME FOR MARY ANN EVANS

What if Grandma Moses had never revisited her childhood dream of painting? That wasn't a skill she suddenly began at the age of seventy-eight; art had always been a part of her life.

What if Amelia Earhart gave up being a woman willing to break out of traditional roles?

What if a little girl born in poverty in rural Mississippi never took her ad-lib talents into the talk show arena to become the phenomenon we know as Oprah Winfrey?

I encourage you to step out of the shadow. Step into the light of your own brilliance. Shine and be seen for the gift you are to this world.

Know that you are making a difference in this world by being your unique self and live your life with all the love, compassion, and creativity you can cram into it. Follow your dreams and share your gifts and talents with the world.

Let yourself experience what is possible for you. Be curious about those fleeting thoughts that you dismiss so readily. Lean into those thoughts and ask, "What's next?"

—Daily inspiration by Mary E. Knippel, Writer Unleashed

27.

August Nights

In August, in Canada, the heat explodes, and we enjoy laughter and hot dogs.

Cold drinks prepared with ice cubes, and maybe a splash of joy.

I am inspired by the illuminated nights. The fire embers pop and hiss into the sky above—a sky that seems so clear just above the horizon.

The moments that we hold on to until the dusk returns to dawn. In August, I am grateful for the little things. I find they mean the most.

What are you grateful for? A warm night, cool breeze, special moments, a starry sky, a beautiful sunset, or magnificent sunrise? Today, pause and reflect on what you are truly grateful for.

—Daily inspiration by Leigh Bursey, Musician, Speaker, and Municipal Councillor

28.

Slow Down

Where did the summer go? It always flies by, no matter how we try to savor each day. As we prepare for the start of school and to begin the rat race once again, it is more important than ever to slow down. This month it is so easy to lose focus and become overwhelmed.

Slow down!

One day at a time, one minute at a time, one breath at a time.

Life is not a race, and there is no trophy. So, try not to become inundated with everything all at once and take the time to enjoy each day. Take a moment today to stop, pause, breathe, and richly embrace this moment just for you.

—*Daily inspiration by Dr. Sarah Breen*

29.

Thought for the Day

"Problems are not stop signs, they are guidelines."
—ROBERT SCHULLER

30.

How Do You Become More Visible?

You might hear from people that you need to be more visible in your business. You may believe it's a wonderful idea. But how do you start?

1. Make a plan.

2. Bring in support.

3. Be consistent in implementing the plan.

Your plan doesn't have to be perfect—but you must have something set down to move you forward. Your plan is the set of activities you need to do to help yourself to be seen, just like you have plans for your other goals like business sales, vacations, and events. Just get started; you can shift or tweak your plan along the way.

You don't have to go it alone—life is not a solo journey. Work with a coach or mentor to develop a plan that will help you strategically build your visibility and reach your goals. Bring in support in the form of friends or team members to keep you inspired and on target.

Consistency is key. In our business and our lives, we need to make sure that we are consistent in how we show up in the world. Leaning in, then not following up, responding, then hiding, or constantly shifting your plans will *not* work.

Decide to be *all in* your willingness to be visible, to *bloom*, and to *shine*, and you'll be well on your way to success!

—Daily inspiration by Rebecca Hall Gruyter, Influencer and Empowerment Leader

31.

Thirsty

"You can lead a horse to water, but you cannot make them drink."

"You can make them thirsty to want to drink."

—DR. CHERYLISM

This is my favorite corollary to this often-used saying. This saying is all about control. You cannot make someone do something they are not willing or able to do. Many people stop here, however, and they stop too soon. Particularly, as a business coach and educator in higher ed, my role is to make my students and clients *want* to drink. Give someone a fish, and they only eat for today. Teach someone how, and they will know how to quench their own hunger and thirst for a lifetime. The goal is self-sufficiency. Motivation is not easy. You simply have to show them another way forward, so they will trust you enough to join you at the watering hole.

—Daily inspiration by Dr. Cheryl Lentz, The Academic Entrepreneur

September

1.

Keeping Busy in What Brings You Joy

Do you know people who just seem to be everywhere, doing everything effortlessly, with lots of joyful energy? You might find yourself wondering why you can't be like them. You wonder if you are enough. You feel bogged down in tasks facing you that do not feel joyful at all.

I used to do, do, do until I became stressed out and burned out. People thought I was "that person," but in fact, I was definitely missing the joy! Until I learned some important lessons about self-nourishment. Here are practices that have helped me stay joyful and balanced:

I find things that bring me joy and having them in my life is non-negotiable. I start every day with routines that give me a boost and keep me centered.

If I find that I begin to be that former stressed-out creature, I've learned to pause right there before it gets too far and breathe deeply (stress has us breathing too shallowly).

I might take a timeout or a break, doing something that will bring me back to joy.

When I am making a decision, I always run it by questions like: Is this going to make the path easier for another? Will this help someone else bloom and share their talents and gifts?

What practices are you building into your daily life to support, center, and nourish you?

—Daily inspiration by Rebecca Hall Gruyter, Influencer and Empowerment Leader

2.

Thought for the Day

"Our daily decisions and habits have a huge impact upon both our levels of happiness and success."

—SHAWN ACHOR

3.

Thought for the Day

"The two most important days in your life are the day you are born and the day you find out why."

—MARK TWAIN

4.

Let Your New Self Bloom and Shine

You've made it. Look outside—notice most trees are giving their best fruits to all creatures. You cannot succeed in this journey alone. Giving allows others to experience something new to come alongside you. Share your vision and goals with those you respect and those for whom you have high esteem—your family and friends. Balance is the foundation for good health in everything in life. Balance is the foundation for peace, harmony, beauty, health, wellness, wellbeing, and much more. Moderation in everything you do is the practical term for balance. Don't deprive yourself from or indulge into too much of anything, and always **remember to recenter yourself back to your core principles. Let your new self bloom and shine.**

Your identity is only polished and strengthened when you interact with others. **You, as a person, find full value only in the presence of others.** It is a lot better and easier when your immediate circle is made of individuals with higher and noble goals, similar interests, and complementary skills. **When different notes of music collectively complement one another, they create a pleasant sound called a melody.** Human melody is what you should look for in your unions and associations with others. What notes are you bringing to the music of life?

—*Daily inspiration by Fabien W. Edjou, Author & Life Coach*

5.

Thought for the Day

"A relationship that is truly genuine does not keep changing its colors. Real gold never rusts. If a relationship is really solid and golden, it will be unbreakable. Not even Time can destroy its shine."

—SUZY KASSEM

6.

Better Communication, Deeper Connection

"Your connection with others is only as strong as your communication with others."

—DR. KIMBERLY SCHEHRER

Much of my work with teens and parents involves communicating better with each other. Here are some lessons I've learned about communication.

Communication is a two-way street. One person is expressing the message, and the other person is receiving it. The desired result of communication is for our messages to be received to get our needs and wants met, acknowledge our perspectives, and/or to convey our feelings.

When we are reacting, we are not listening. In an emotional state, we tend to react without hearing the other person's side. This only puts the other person on the defensive and actually escalates the behavior that we are reacting to, which, in turn, triggers more reaction from us.

Do we communicate to be heard or to be right? Often, we communicate to be "right" rather than allow for negotiation, compromise, or simply to agree to disagree. Being "right" means being judgmental, which blocks the opening for a new idea or perspective to enter.

Active listening is an important component of communication. This means being fully present with the other person with empathy and an honest desire to understand where the other person stands.

Words have power; they can save a life, harm a life, and change the world. Perhaps the most important lesson of all! How empowering would it be for others, especially young people, to hear us being intentional and purposeful with our words?

Let's practice being truly present and connected in our conversations.

—*Daily inspiration by Dr. Kimberly Schehrer, Teen Breakthrough Expert*

7.

Thought for the Day

"Many of life's failures are people who did not realize how close they were to success when they gave up."

—THOMAS A. EDISON

8.

Thought for the Day

"Believe that your life is not ordinary and never look down on what you can do to impact a life."

—SUNDAY ADELAJA

9.

What the World Needs Is More of You

I believe every single person has been given unique talents, abilities, gifts, and dreams. My vision is for everyone to have the chance to show up in just the way they are gifted to serve.

The world needs *you* in all your unique and wonderful ways!

I envision a big, beautiful gift box that I am handing to you right now. It is filled with reminders of who you are, how wonderful you are, and the many ways that the world needs *you*. Take a moment to think about what it is inside the box—all the things that you love about yourself and others love about you, all the things that you were brought here to give to the world!

Take another moment to think about the joy and fun you have had—with your friends, with loved ones, or all by yourself (which is a precious gift itself). Laughter and joy are present-moment experiences that bring our world together. The world can never have enough of our joy and laughter. The world can never have enough of *you*! **Remember to share the gift of you!**

—Daily inspiration by Rebecca Hall Gruyter, Influencer and Empowerment Leader

10.

You Are Valuable

Zoe Kravitz, model and actress, quotes, "Beauty is when you can appreciate yourself. When you can love yourself, that's when you're the most beautiful."

Research shows that self-acceptance leads to greater satisfaction with your life. It is time to love and accept yourself for the wonder that you are.

You deserve to be loved and romanced by the best person in the world, and that is you. You need to treat yourself to soft music, candles, a bubble bath, and a glass of your favorite beverage. As you are enjoying the moment, relax and reflect and say, "I am someone special. I have strength and courage that I never knew. I'm not the same person I once was, and I'm proud of who I am becoming. Today, I choose to love me and believe in myself. I will take care of me. I am worth it."

It's not always easy to learn to love and believe in yourself. It's time to shake self-negativity and embrace our uniqueness. It's okay to pray and be shown the way. You will be shown **there is no one else in the world like you; you are special and rare.** All of life's best is yours. Remember to take wonderful care of you.

—*Daily inspiration by Toni Stone Bruce, Precious Stones 4 Life, LLC*

11.

Thought for the Day

"Always strive to do the right thing even when it isn't a popular choice. By doing so, you become a better person."

—TORRON-LEE DEWAR

12.

Thought for the Day

"You don't have to remind a flower when its time to bloom is near; it has been preparing for it all of its life."

—MATSHONA DHLIWAYO

13.

Self-Worth

The comparison game. It's a soul-killer and a joy-stealer.

And yet we are so prone to it – always measuring ourselves against others. Wondering if we measure up. Asking if we have what it takes. Social media and the constant thrum of information coming at us online has only heightened the stakes. Now we're not just comparing our lives, but we're comparing our unrealistic, virtual lives.

No good can come of it. In fact, studies show that it's killing us. Either we judge ourselves and our curated lives more highly than others, and we approach our relationships with pride. Or we find ourselves to be "less than" and loathe our inadequacies.

What if, instead, we could settle the question of our worth? Without comparing it to anyone else. Can you imagine a world where we are freed up to learn from each other with nothing to prove? To say, "Oh, what a great idea" without feeling that pang of inadequacy that comes because we didn't think of it first? Or to cheer each other on in life? **Your worth doesn't come from being better than someone else. It comes from being you, created in the image of a good God. How can you embrace that today?**

—*Daily inspiration by Shannon McKee, Author, Mentor, and Life Coach*

14.

How Your Ancestors Teach You to *Shine*

I am fortunate to have had wonderful relationships with four grand-mothers who richly blessed me and impacted my life. They each, in their own way, inspired the shape and form of the work I get to do in the world.

When, as a child, I didn't feel very good about myself, one grandmother taught me to give myself the same grace, love, and understanding as I would for my very best friend. Another taught me not to wait for permission but to step into who I am authentically and powerfully. From another, I learned to work hard for what truly matters to me and always to walk with honor and integrity. And another taught me the importance of lifting others up and how we can all make a positive difference, heart by heart and life by life.

I'm thankful for their legacy and the gift of having them in my life. I think with wonder about what each of my grandmothers learned from *their* elders in ways that influenced the persons they would become—and on and on, back through time, each generation standing on the shoulders of the one before them!

Who in your life has influenced and inspired you along your journey? Take a moment now to think about them, celebrate them, and send your love and gratitude their way. **We don't walk alone on this journey, and the more we open ourselves up to remembering those who walked beside us, the more we bring out their powerful gifts to guide us.**

—*Daily inspiration by Rebecca Hall Gruyter, Influencer and Empowerment Leader*

15.

Happiness

"Learn how to be happy with what you have
while you pursue all that you want."

—JIM ROHN

Be grateful for all that you are right now. Instead of lamenting where you are in your life, accept what is, and if you want to change something to be more in alignment with your true self, take inspired action. Inspired action stems from being happy. Happiness begins when you look for things that make your heart smile. The smell of the earth after a rain, the radiant colors of blooming flowers, a beautiful sunset, the sound of birds chirping and children laughing, the taste of your favorite food, the feeling of a cat purring on your lap, or the joy that you feel when your dog greets you at the door can all be catalysts for your happiness, if you let them. These things may seem small and inconsequential, but they are building blocks to your happiness. It's up to you to choose to let the little things in your life that are present everywhere to inspire you. Like a ray of sunshine, as you allow yourself to feel happiness, it will illuminate your path. Let your happiness guide your choices, and instead of fear, and you will reap the pleasure of manifesting your desires. Choose to allow your inner happiness to bloom in the service of your dreams!

—*Daily inspiration by Kimi Avary, MA, Relationship Navigation Specialist*

16.

Thought for the Day

"The pessimist sees difficulty in every opportunity. The optimist sees opportunity in every difficulty."

—WINSTON CHURCHILL

17.

Creatively Energize Your Dreams

During this transition from restful summer into fall routines, fond memories linger in my mind of "retreat season" at the church where I worked years ago. Each autumn, one particularly memorable quote shared during those weekends away tangoed in my mind:

> *"Vision without action is merely a dream.*
> *Action without vision just passes the time.*
> *Vision with action can change the world."*
>
> —JOEL A. BARKER

Over time, it rang truer for me. "*Doing*" (masculine energy) and "*being*" (feminine energy) are EQUALLY important forces for life in the world around us, and within us. Most of us, however, lean into one or the other, depending on our comfort zone. When I speak on this topic, the "dreamers" in the audience often prefer to overlook structure, time, details, and deadlines. The "doers," on the other hand, bristle at the idea of pausing for stillness, introspection, and "mind-body-soul" check-ins. The problem is that too much "doing," *or* too much "dreaming" might be causing you burnout or disconnection. If so, your dreams remain only dreams. Your actions carry on without meaning or purpose. Nothing changes. Hope dwindles. However, **when you discover how to balance "doing" and "being," cherished dreams start to come true almost magically.** Is your dream on track to come true this year? What energy shift do you need to make this month to succeed? Learning how to manage and integrate your "doing" and "being" life energy is a simple yet powerful way to bloom and *shine*!

—**Daily inspiration by Marlene Elizabeth, author of Moneywings™**

18.

What Time Is It?

*"Know when to hold 'em, know when to fold 'em,
know when to walk away, know when to run."*

—"THE GAMBLER" BY KENNY ROGERS

This is one of my favorite leadership theories by none other than country music legend, Kenny Rogers. **Knowledge is as important as knowing when to step in, step up, or step out.** Sometimes the best decision is to do nothing. Sometimes the best decision is to wait. Sometimes the best decision is to walk away and live to fight another day. Wisdom and experience will help us get it right, more often, the first time. Think about all possible outcomes and the opportunity cost of doing something, only doing a little bit, or doing nothing. Take the time to explore tools in your toolkit to ensure the use of the most effective tool for the most effective outcome. Take time to check-in and evaluate. Is it time to stop? Time to lean in and do more? Time to listen? Time to walk away? Time to listen to the answer and follow it? What time is it?

—*Daily inspiration by Dr. Cheryl Lentz, The Academic Entrepreneur*

19.

Thought for the Day

"Greater love has no one than this, that someone lay down his life for his friends."

—JOHN 15:13

20.

Thought for the Day

If you set goals and go after them with all the determination you can muster, your gifts will take you places that will amaze you.

–LES BROWN

21.

Choose What Matters Most

Do you let yourself be poured into by the things that help, nourish, and support you to **shine**?

Or are you letting other things, perhaps other people's priorities, become your priority? It's so easy to get "too busy," become overwhelmed, and not be able to complete the priorities we set for that day. Does this sound familiar to you?

Part of the challenge is that we are so good at continuing to add things to our plate! We're talented, we want to give and to serve, and we want to say "yes" to so many things and people.

This is a good time to stop and check-in.

Take just thirty seconds. Write down what you currently have on your plate. Make a list of what you have now, what's coming up, what needs to be finished, and what needs to be started.

Now, look at your list and notice: What feels heavy? What feels pressured? What doesn't? It's good to know where you are feeling pulled or depleted instead of feeling poured into.

Reset your "shoulds." It is very disempowering to say, "I have to, I should, I need to..." If you find yourself thinking those words, shift it to "I choose."

Now choose what matters most to help you move forward. We can get caught up in doing lots of things and forget to choose to do the most important ones to help us move forward on our goals.

Because, in reality, you are choosing all the time. You are empowered with the choice to do the things that serve you and let you shine ever brighter. Choose to *shine* and fully share the gift of you!

—Daily inspiration by Rebecca Hall Gruyter, Influencer and Empowerment Leader

22.

Your Story Matters

"To love oneself is the beginning of a lifelong romance."

—OSCAR WILDE

I'm curious: are you involved in a great romance, a grand passion?

Or are you living someone else's life? You know, the one everybody else thinks you are perfect for, instead of following your dream?

Perhaps you have you identified your bliss, yet hesitate for fear those close to you who won't understand.

Well, I'll let you in on a little secret: they don't have to understand, or get it, because it isn't their story. It's yours!

Your story matters! Because it is exactly that: your story. It belongs only to you and not to anyone else.

You matter!

You hold the key to unlocking your story—the story of how you've overcome life's challenges as a legacy to future generations. The important thing to remember is that you are connecting with who needs to hear from you. People are waiting and hungry for what you have to say. Yes, I do mean you. No one else can tell your story.

You are the central character, and your story matters! Now tell us: what's your story?

23.

Thought for the Day

"Do all the good you can, for all the people you can, in all the ways you can, as long as you can."

—HILLARY CLINTON

24.

Choose Happiness

Choose Happiness by Releasing Anger and Forgiving Others.

The main reason to forgive others is not for the benefit of the forgiven, but rather for the benefit of the forgiver. A person cannot be happy and angry at the same time. If we hold grudges and foster anger, we make ourselves miserable. It is an unpleasant way to live. When you hold onto grudges, hurt, and pain and let anger roost in you, the person that suffers the most is you. The target of your anger is often oblivious while you walk around in an unpleasant state. Choose happiness for your own sake.

—Daily inspiration by Patrick P. Long, International Best-Selling Author

25.

Thought for the Day

"We must believe that we are gifted for something, and that this thing, at whatever cost, must be attained."

—MARIE CURIE

26.

Words

My best friend since childhood was going through a violent and messy divorce. At the time, I offered a few simple words of encouragement. Years later, she told me it was these words I told her that pulled her through. I never realized the power of my own words.

Your words matter. Choose your words mindfully, purposefully, and from the heart when you talk to others and yourself. They can have a lasting impact.

Let's have our impact be positive.

—Daily inspiration by Maureen Ryan Blake, Founder and Principal of The Power of the Tribe

27.

Where Are You Showing Up?
Where Are You Shrinking Back?

I often tell my clients how important it is to just *show up* in our imperfect perfections, just where we are in this moment. It is not always easy, as there are going to be times when we want to shrink back instead of showing up.

It can be easy to join something—a networking community, social media group, or online group program—with enthusiasm, then you find yourself missing meetings, not responding, and not following up with connections. Has that ever happened to you? If so, I encourage you to:

• **Check-in** on where you are with something you have joined; explore where you are showing up and where you have been shrinking back. Notice with curiosity and explore why.

• **Take a good look to decide if this is the right fit now.** Your time and energy are precious; your gifts are precious, and the world is waiting to receive them. If it doesn't feel in alignment anymore, then make the preparations to leave. Sometimes things are just for a season.

• **If you decide to continue with the experience,** celebrate, and explore ways that you can lean in and enjoy, give, and receive even more.

Realize that the world misses out on your contribution when you shrink back. This is why you want to really find those things of value to you that nourish you to *bloom*, support you on an ongoing basis, and for which you can make the commitment to show up, contribute, and *shine*.

—Daily inspiration by Rebecca Hall Gruyter, Influencer and Empowerment Leader

28.

September Moments

In September, I start to feel that the long days of sunlight don't last quite long enough. The heat begins to cool, and we make subtle preparations for what is yet to come.

I observe the beautiful falling leaves, so vibrant and limitless. In their last moments of living and breathing, they blow freely, decorating our lawns and sidewalks as we subtly attempt to hold on to their smell.

In September, I draw inspiration from the new collage of memories that summer gifted me. I am grateful for the calm before the winter storm—the opportunity to stop and reflect, to prepare and look forward to the winter and the holidays.

—Daily inspiration by Leigh Bursey, Musician, Speaker, and Municipal Councillor

29.

Thought for the Day

"Darkness enables us to shine."

—STEVEN MAGEE

30.

Change

Fall is in the air! You can immediately feel the shift. All of a sudden, the mornings have a crisp bite to them, even though the days are still warm. The routine is back, yet everything feels new. It is time to enjoy the beauty of fall—the leaves changing colors, the apple orchards, and even pumpkins start to make their way back into our lives. Do you embrace this change? Or are you afraid of the winter to come? **Lean into fall. Lean into the magic of the beauty that lives in these changes. Lean into the beauty of change in your own life.** Do not fear what can be. Are you ready to fall into something new? Embrace the beauty and wonder of change today.

—*Daily inspiration by Dr. Sarah Breen*

October

1.

"Now" – The True Gift of Time.

October is the beginning of the end of a cycle. You have witnessed, experienced, and learned so much. Look back and reminisce on your entire journey thus far. Look back to learn as much as possible from your journey. Remember, most people don't know the true notion of time. In fact, there is only one time in life for every creature, and that time is now. Just as you cannot go back one step in time and change anything that happened yesterday, you are equally unable to move forward one step in time into the future. The same is true for the previous hour and the next hour; the previous minute and the next minute; the previous second and the next second. The only point of connection with time for everyone is always now.

"Now" is truly a gift of time, literally called "present." It is not just present as time, but it is a present as a gift. Everyone only lives one moment at a time, and once a moment is missed, you are left with regrets. The time was, is, and will always be the same as now; it doesn't change and will never change simply because it is perfect. We are the ones constantly changing during our journey inside time. We mark our progress in time by measuring how far and how long we've traveled. How are you choosing to spend your present moment?

—*Daily inspiration by Fabien W. Edjou, Author & Life Coach*

2.

Thought for the Day

"You can overcome whatever is going on around you if you believe in the light that lives within you."

—JUSTINE EDWARD

3.

Transforming Challenges into Growth

"Resilient people do not bounce back from hard experiences; they find healthy ways to integrate them into their lives.... people find that great calamity met with great spirit can create great strength."

—DAVID SCHROEDER

Here is my definition of resilience: *transforming challenges into growth*. Life will have challenges, that is certain. But **when you have resilience, the bumps in the road have a different spin for you**, because you know you will reach your destination in spite of them. In fact, those bumps will help you grow, bloom, and thrive!

Have you ever been in the middle of a situation in which you thought you might never get out of it, or you would never recover from it? But you did—you're here today to tell the tale!

You now look back and realize you *did* recover and, in fact, became stronger and better because of it.

The key to resilience is *how* we bounce back. Gritting your teeth and persevering is one way, but a much more sustainable method of bouncing back is to transform your adversity into self-growth. Resilience helps us to get up again and move forward in those areas that are most important to us.

This is what I teach the teens I work with, and they find that their thoughts shift from: It has to be a struggle; that's just how it is, so get used to it! to: I get to think of this setback as an opportunity for something better.

Different feeling, isn't it? And I guarantee, a different outcome.

—Daily inspiration by Dr. Kimberly Schehrer, Teen Breakthrough Expert

4.

Thought for the Day

"The purpose of our lives is to be happy."

—DALAI LAMA

5.

You Were Made for Such a Time as This, Therefore, *Shine*!

"If not now, when?"

—HILLEL, THE ELDER

Things happen in our lives that we don't expect and certainly didn't choose—a car accident, a divorce, a job loss, or illness. "Such a time as this" could be an opportunity. We may not have chosen the event, but **we can choose how we are going to respond: to suffer or *shine*!**

These times may have us answering questions we don't often answer until we're faced with the possible end of ourselves. These are times when we get to ask **what matters most to us and how do we make that move forward and serve us?**

Life events challenge us to respond from an empowered place, to rethink things, and to realize that time is precious.

Wherever you are in your journey, wherever you're being called, remember, it's now, it's today. Tomorrow isn't guaranteed. We have now.

What action can you take today to help you move forward that matters most to you?

—Daily inspiration by Rebecca Hall Gruyter, Influencer and Empowerment Leader

6.

Thought for the Day

"In order to succeed you must fail, so that you know what not to do the next time."

—ANTHONY J. D'ANGELO

7.

Shine Your Light Today

"Each time I write a book, every time I face that yellow pad, I think, 'Uh, oh, they're going to find out now. I've run a game on everybody, and they're going to find me out.'"

—MAYA ANGELOU

I am a writer. It's taken me a lifetime to say that simple declarative sentence because I've had that same self-doubt expressed above by the celebrated author, Maya Angelou. So, if you are like me, we are in very good company. Yes, at times, it is hard to hear your soul's whispers when that other voice challenges, "Who do you think you are?" And, "Who would want to hear from you anyway?"

It's what we do after that voice whispers that is important.

When I show up at the page, I'm writing to understand as well as to be understood.

I am positive there are plenty of kindred souls who would want to hear what you or I have to say.

Okay. I can just see you shaking your head and vowing that nothing important has happened to you. Maybe you didn't invent a gadget or write the great American novel. However, you are designed to live a life that is exquisitely your own. And when you do that, you are sharing your gifts and having an impact on the world. You will have said something of value.

Shine your light today. Share your gifts with the world.

—Daily inspiration by Mary E. Knippel, Writer Unleashed

8.

Thought for the Day

*"Mediocrity will never do. You are
capable of something better."*

—GORDON B. HINCKLEY

9.

Mask

Ghosts and goblins, witches and scarecrows. Halloween is coming. Scary stories and haunted houses, but there is nothing to fear. **Maybe it is time to think about taking off your mask**. What are you hiding? What are you afraid to show the world? Are you afraid the world will reject your true self? Why do you care so much?

Perhaps my biggest challenge is caring too much about the opinion of others. It is something I struggle with daily, and maybe you do as well. The world is massive, and we are but a small part, so be yourself. Let's take our masks we use to shield our true selves. Let's really, truly connect and share the unique gift of who we are with each other. True connection, true sharing, no mask required.

Take off your mask because that is what makes you, you.

—*Daily inspiration by Dr. Sarah Breen*

10.

Thought for the Day

*Hardships often prepare ordinary people
for an extraordinary destiny.*

—C.S. LEWIS

11.

Into the Unknown

When life presses you toward new horizons you seek
and your "heart is willing (but your flesh is weak)"
to answer the call, to just take a peek
into the great unknown...
Breathe. Don't "over" think.
Trust your intuition, and *believe.*
Yes, around the bend you probably can't see
what lies ahead, where the dusty road leads;
But take comfort, rest a bit more at ease:
God is already there painting fall leaves
(it's been one month, or two, even 4 months at least!)
Are you feeling a season of change, new possibility in your bones?
A whisper saying, "It's time to dream *big*, bloom, SHINE, *grow*"?
What if the unknown revealed your "north star"? Or genius zone?
Inspired you to unmask the beautiful gift you are?
Empowered you to live financially free, as the one who borrows loans?
Motivating others by your example to fear *less*, enjoy more
adventures told.
Be safe; don't settle for less treasure than your heart can hold.
The only place where the "sky's the limit" and character unfolds
(and, surprisingly, where you'll feel far less alone)
...is into the unknown.

—Daily inspiration by Marlene Elizabeth, author of Moneywings™

12.

Thought for the Day

"God has made you just the way you are to impact others right where he's placed you."

—TIM HILLER

13.

Harvest

"A thankful receiver bears a plentiful harvest."

—WILLIAM BLAKE

In today's world, most of us are less connected with the seasons, in harvesting summer's bounty, and we often forget to "harvest" the blessings in our lives. In every experience, there are always hidden blessings. Sometimes they are buried under the biggest challenges or tragedies. There may be twists and turns that, at the moment, have you shaking your head in dismay but, in hindsight, make sense.

We imagine life is supposed to be a straight line with a clear destination, but it's not. It's more like a twisted spaghetti noodle where seemingly disconnected experiences wind together to give you the right pieces of your unique puzzle.

You can trust your soul has a destination for you, even if you cannot see it yet. Set aside some time and ponder the blessings in your life. Ask yourself, "What is the blessing in this situation that I have been unable to see?" **By taking stock and pondering how something could actually be a blessing in disguise, you'll begin to see the gifts. Be thankful for all the blessings that your life has to offer.**

—Daily inspiration by Kimi Avary, MA, Relationship Navigation Specialist

14.

Unlocking Your Prosperity

We might not remember when or where we first heard messages about money, but somewhere along the way, we internalized them and accepted them as truth. These "truths" then became part of our money stories and shaped the way we feel and think about money. The myths become part of our relationship with money.

One myth is that it's bad to focus on money, and only greedy people are concerned with money. This untruth makes us feel guilty or ashamed for wanting to be financially successful.

The truth is that you can have money—lots of it—and still be serving and living in alignment with who you are! Money can be used for good things or for not-good things. The paper dollars and metal coins that we call "money" are absolutely neutral. If you look for it, you can find proof that money is good, that it is okay to focus on money, and that people who do are giving and doing amazing good in the world.

What you choose to do with money—how you define its importance in your own life—is where the power of money can be used to bring about good or evil. That choice is up to you!

What myths about money might you believe that are holding you back from reaching your full potential?

—Daily inspiration by Rebecca Hall Gruyter, Influencer and Empowerment Leader

15.

Responsible for You

Take Primary Responsibility for You.

While my wife was battling cancer, the battle brought myriad challenges and hardships into our lives, accumulating stress, which brought many thoughts and feelings to the surface. We never felt supported by one another. I recognized that my wife did support me in many ways, yet something was missing. Something I could never identify. During the biggest fight we ever had, it hit me. I didn't just want her to agree to invest money in something or give me time to work on an endeavor. I wanted her to believe in me and be excited by what I was doing. She couldn't.

I learned that neither of us was right nor wrong. We just had different tolerances, and she couldn't stand the risks of entrepreneurship. **This led to a greater understanding that no one completes you.** That idea sounds great for romantic movies, but even your closest partner can't fill all your gaps. In fact, neither can you. We all have shortcomings, weaknesses, and intolerances. This is why we look for inspirations throughout our lives and why we benefit from others' stories. When I took primary responsibility for myself, it made me stronger. I needed that strength. My wife passed from her cancer a couple of years later, and I'd be left to raise our four young children. **Empowered by these lessons, I'm more capable of carrying on. I had already learned to take primary responsibility for me, which has helped tremendously.**

—*Daily inspiration by Patrick P. Long, International Best-Selling Author*

16.

Thought for the Day

"My mission in life is not merely to survive, but to thrive; and to do so with some passion, some compassion, some humor, and some style"

—MAYA ANGELOU

17.

You Are Right

"As a man thinketh, so he is."

—NAPOLEON HILL

Napoleon Hill understood the psyche of human nature and thus understood the world of business in ways as few do. Perspective and attitude are everything. **If we think we'll succeed, we will; if we think we will fail, we will. Either way, we are *always* right.** Thus, the lesson is to guard our thoughts and choose wisely to ensure we end up exactly where we want to go. Believe in yourself—even in the face of adversity and even when no one else does—and you will find yourself in a position of strength and success because of the positioning of your thoughts in the process. Be mindful of your thoughts and what you are choosing to believe. You've got this.

—*Daily inspiration by Dr. Cheryl Lentz, The Academic Entrepreneur*

18.

Thought for the Day

"When I was 5 years old, my mother always told me that happiness was the key to life. When I went to school, they asked me what I wanted to be when I grew up. I wrote down 'happy'. They told me I didn't understand the assignment, and I told them they didn't understand life."

—JOHN LENNON

19.

Thought for the Day

"Our greatest fear should not be of failure but of succeeding at things in life that don't really matter."

—FRANCIS CHAN

20.

Thought for the Day

"When everything seems to be going against you, remember that the airplane takes off against the wind, not with it."

—HENRY FORD

21.

Body Check

Our body is the home we carry around twenty-four hours a day, every year from birth to death. That's a sobering thought, as **our health determines the quality of our life.** Many seniors have declared how they should have taken better care of their bodies in their youth by eating healthy, drinking water, exercising, and getting eight hours of sleep. Due to our choices, we suffer from the lack of consideration we have given to our mind, our body, and, ultimately, our spirit.

Sometimes, we treat our bodies as a workhorse plowing a field, pushing it more and working it harder, until we nearly destroy our body and mind.

We can begin by checking in and seeing if we need/want to make a lifestyle change, perhaps to eat more vegetables, fruits, grains, and drinking more water. It's time to put down the remote, get off the couch, and hit the ground walking each day. It's time to start exercising at home or in the gym. Remember to rest and have downtime. Reading daily to inspire our minds and gain wisdom is necessary to keep our emotional and mental capacities alert and full of vigor.

It's time to be our best, respect our bodies, and feed our souls.

—Daily inspiration by Toni Stone Bruce, Precious Stones 4 Life, LLC

22.

Thought for the Day

"In tough times will you whine or shine?"
—DAREN MARTIN

23.

October Inspirations

In October, we pay tribute to the ghosts, monsters, and ghouls. We feed them full of kindness with sweetened, spooky foods. We laugh and scream at movies meant to make our senses tingle. We dress in goofy costumes and drink potions as we mingle.

We collect our favorite characters for slasher film date nights. We homage the creepy darkness while building memories full of light.

We cackle, and we dance and enter contests for the best spook. We supervise our children and help them separate their loot.

All the while, creating moments where memories come from. Holding hands and dressing up and sharing in our love—harmony and community, unity in games.

In October, I am inspired by a childhood that I wished would never end. I am grateful for mischief with my friends.

What inspires you today? What do you celebrate and enjoy in October? Friends? Memories? Special treats or traditions? What are you choosing to be or to do to inspire yourself and others?

—Daily inspiration by Leigh Bursey, Musician, Speaker, and Municipal Councillor

24.

Thought for the Day

"Fearlessness is like a muscle. I know from my own life that the more I exercise it the more natural it becomes to not let my fears run me."

—ARIANNA HUFFINGTON

25.

Turquoise = A Brighter Day

Inspiring others is a fulfilling mission and purpose. While attending a mediumship group, a reader asked me what turquoise means. My response was it is my favorite color. She shared there would be more information in the upcoming weeks.

I heard my angels say, "Wear turquoise to brighten your day." After surveying ideas, my slogan became "Brighten your day with turquoise."

Turquoise is an inspiring and supporting color. I researched the color to understand it better. I discovered this color lightens and brightens your day. It lifts your spirit and moves you in a positive direction.

My mission became to speak about mental illness and the stigma behind it. This excited me because it's a serious health issue and important to portray reality. I want to bring encouragement and light to those that suffer from a mental illness.

Do you ever feel anxious or depressed like you would never get past it? With the pandemic, many people have felt these symptoms. Imagine feeling that non-stop. This is a simple explanation of how mental illness can feel.

If you are feeling low, disheartened, or discouraged, please put on something turquoise to help support you. Please send positive energy for those of us that struggle with mental illnesses, as many are feeling this way all the time.

If you also struggle, there are many outlets to find support. You can find more information on my website, https://www.catherinemlaub.com/turquoise/.

—Daily inspiration by Catherine M. Laub, Podcast Host

26.

Remember Who You Are

Remember who you are, remember your birthright, remember the quickening of your spirit when you're in joy and in alignment. There's real power in that. When we step into remembering who we are, there's a strength about it that we can feel that helps us feel grounded in those times when we feel pulled in all directions or taking care of others and forgetting to pay attention to ourselves.

Let's take it a step further. Throughout these days and weeks, tap into this powerful awareness and put out your antenna to tune into noticing:

"What is more of who I am?"

"What am I being called to bring forth?"

When you ask these questions, know that the answer is inside you, waiting to respond. It sometimes is just about tuning in and remembering because you knew it all along. I encourage you to actively look out for that and be prepared for some exciting, clarifying answers to help you step forward.

When we're willing to strip that away and say, "This is me," we find our energy increases, and people really lean in and connect.

—Daily inspiration by Rebecca Hall Gruyter, Influencer and Empowerment Leader

27.

Breathe

Breathe, just breathe.

So often, I get caught up in life. At this time, we get to stop and just breathe. Take a moment for you to just be and breathe.

—Daily inspiration by Maureen Ryan Blake, Founder and Principal of The Power of the Tribe

28.

Thought for the Day

*"Too many of us are not living our dreams
because we are living our fears."*

—LES BROWN

29.

Pass the Garlic Bread

We weren't just eating. We were feasting on life.

From the loud, four-year-old "Mama" called out from one end of the table to the other (he wanted to show her he could make the letter "V") to the cousin giggles and Mad Lib games to the ribbing between brothers-in-law-become-friends to the folding-in of a few more who are just like family... It was a feast in the truest sense of the word. "Pass the garlic bread" was really code for "pass the love." Pass the laughter and the pleasure of being together. Pass the common-bond that ties us even tighter.

There is something about sharing a table, isn't there? One author has called it "table life." It's a dying art in American culture, but I think it's one we need to hold onto because of moments like these.

Yes, pass the garlic bread. Pass it over and over again, please! Till I'm stuffed. Fill me up with these moments that nourish my soul.

—*Daily inspiration by Shannon McKee, Author, Mentor, and Life Coach*

30.

Thought for the Day

"When life gets you down do you wanna know what you've gotta do? Just keep swimming!"

—DORY, FINDING NEMO

31.

Making Empowered Choices

"Every problem is a gift—without problems, we would not grow."
—TONY ROBBINS

Your work is your passion and your heart; it taps into your deepest talents and purpose, and you feel blessed to be allowed to do this for a living! You hop out of bed (at least most mornings) to go to work and serve as you are called.

Then things seem to get more complex, and what you were doing yesterday isn't always working today. Your work begins to feel more like a burden than a joy. What might be happening is a growth step—how exciting! This means that it is time to pull back from the weeds, to step back and explore:

What am I building?

What actions do I need to take?

What do I need to delegate?

What are the high-level decisions that I need to make?

I have found that you really can't move forward with your important growth strategies *until* you recognize exactly where your business stands. These questions will help you get clearer about what is yours to do next. Once you have the answers (for yourself or with your people), you can begin to get strategic about your direction, delegating and hiring, and adjusting programs and systems that will meet your new growth goals.

You can make empowered choices in business and life for your future when you know where you are and where you are called to go.

—Daily inspiration by Rebecca Hall Gruyter, Influencer and Empowerment Leader

November

1.

Thought for the Day

"Gratitude is the sign of noble souls."

–AESOP

2.

Gratitude Tree

As I write, the reds and golds of November are fading. The trees have released them, and they float to the ground so that their colors now blanket the earth. Crunchy under our feet as we walk to school. Scooped up into great piles for play while the parents rake them to the street.

But there is one lonely tree that has only just begun to show its colors. On Thursday, the buds will open, and the colors will begin a most vibrant week-long display. By week's end, she will be the most beautiful of all trees. Her branches ablaze with Autumn color. Her "leaves" pouring forth praises to the One who brings her branches to life.

We call her the Gratitude Tree.

Her roots reach deep into the fabric of our family. Her leaves are the simple testimonies of grace upon grace. Handwritten notes are hung on the branches as reminders of all the good gifts that we have received this year. A thanksgiving. Before the Thanksgiving.

What are you thankful for that you can hang on your own Gratitude Tree?

—*Daily inspiration by Shannon McKee, Author, Mentor, and Life Coach*

3.

Make Magic During the Holidays

Have you ever experienced this? You host a holiday dinner or party with a lot of people. Your head is filled with all the distractions around the event—the planning, cooking, gifts, attending to guests, family drama, excitement, and laughter. Then, it's over. And you hardly remember any part of it!

An event that was supposed to be memorable instead is a blur. Yes, it's happened to me too—I wasn't fully present in the moment, and those precious moments never had a chance to embed on a cellular level.

My holiday gift to you is this: Before you start something or go to an event, take some moments to stop, breathe, and ask:

"What is it that I need to know or to have today?"

"What is it that will encourage me, equip me, and empower me to bring in my magic?"

"What can I appreciate and celebrate in this moment?"

There is power in stopping and checking in with yourself this way, a strength about it that you can feel that helps keep you grounded, no matter what.

Taking this a powerful step further, ask yourself: **"What is it that I'm willing to receive?"**

—Today, in general, or in regard to the activity or event you are about to experience.) Then open yourself up to connect with the answers. You may be surprised by the magic that happens!

—Daily inspiration by Rebecca Hall Gruyter, Influencer and Empowerment Leader

4.

Thoughts and Feelings

Take Control of Your Thoughts and Feelings Without Remorse.

My wife passed away after a three-and-half-year battle with cancer. I wrote a book about our experiences with her cancer and our life together. The battle and her loss spurred some horrible thoughts and feelings that overwhelmed me at times. I felt guilty about many of these thoughts and feelings. Some of them made me feel like a terrible, selfish person.

The writing of the book forced me to examine these thoughts and feelings deeply. I acknowledged these thoughts and feelings and analyzed them extensively. I came to understand that we often don't control the thoughts and feelings we have. They overwhelm us and are a natural development in times of extreme stress and trauma. **I don't feel guilty about such thoughts and feelings any longer. I've come to learn that while we can't control them initially, we can always control what we do with them.** We can learn from them and shape them into positive action. **Don't dwell on guilt, but rather forge ahead enlightened by the lessons of your experiences and the wisdom you gain along the way.** Choose what you do with these thoughts and feelings. How can you shape them into positive action?

—*Daily inspiration by Patrick P. Long, International Best-Selling Author*

5.

Thought for the Day

"Gratitude is a quality similar to electricity: It must be produced and discharged and used up in order to exist at all."

—WILLIAM FAULKNER

6.

APP—reciate Your Time

After switching from regular coffee to humble decaf, my body did an "I feel good!" happy dance (after recovery, of course, from caffeine underload). This didn't mean, however, that I banished full-strength coffee out of my life forevermore. ("Everything in moderation, including moderation," Irish poet Oscar Wilde quipped.) And so there I sat one chilly morning, car idling in line with all the other local Starbucks Rewards cardholders, inching along minute-by-grueling-minute toward heaven's window—er, I mean, the barista at the drive-through. One might think living only four minutes from this location would mean a ten to fifteen-minute turnaround for a quick cup of a pick-me-up. After arriving home *one hour* later, however—and just in the nick of time before my next client appointment—I thought, *"never will I drink regular coffee like that again! Nope,*

—*I'll order via mobile app.* As I'm sure you agree, dear reader, there is no greater gift than *time*. Here are seven simple time-management tips for a stress-free holiday season for entrepreneurs shared in *Inc.* magazine by CEO and Founder, Marissa Levin:

1. Get offline.

2. Use your auto-responder.

3. Schedule smart (the way an Olympic athlete would approach her training day).

4. Establish boundaries and say no (and choose your events carefully).

5. Know your productivity cycle.

6. Choose a realistic number of tasks and stick with them.

7. Ink it when you think it.

Which time-management tips from the list above, or from other practices you've learned, can help you experience less stress and more ease today?

—*Daily inspiration by Marlene Elizabeth, author of Moneywings™*

7.

The Choices We Make

Even the choices we don't get to make can be stepping stones on the path that leads us to our purpose. Some of those choices that were made for us have been disempowering, abusive, and even dangerous. So, how can they be stepping stones to good things? **I have discovered we can't always choose what happens to us, but we can choose our response.**

As a teenager, the seed of what my purpose would be was planted at a Women of Faith Conference, where I was inspired by the powerful women sharing their stories of hardship, tragedy, and struggle, and how they chose to use their experiences to help and encourage other women. At that moment, I knew I wanted to be a motivational speaker, even though I was so fearful of being visible in any way, shape, or form. I wanted my story and life to be used for good. The seed planted in my heart was that maybe, just maybe, my story could help another. That seed pulled me forward to overcome my fears, and today I have bloomed from the seeds of my purpose planted so long ago!

Perhaps you can relate to not feeling like you have a choice, that others are controlling your life and your destiny, that it's better to hide. **You still have a choice.**

Despite everything that may happen *to* you in your life, you do have at least one choice that is always yours to make. You can *still* be empowered and choose your response today and going forward! Your choices—your responses—can change the path of your life.

All of the things that happen to us can become the fuel that propels us toward our purpose.

—*Daily inspiration by Rebecca Hall Gruyter, Influencer and Empowerment Leader*

8.

Thought for the Day

"For me, every hour is grace. And I feel gratitude in my heart each time I can meet someone and look at his or her smile."

—ELIE WIESEL

9.

Thought for the Day

"When you practice gratefulness, there is a sense of respect towards others."

—DALAI LAMA

10.

Your Life, Your Story

"Don't just write a strong female protagonist. Be one!"

—A. D. POSEY

Another word for protagonist is hero. And, my dear, that is *you!* Day by day, you are writing the story of your life. Whether you are center stage as a speaker or standing alone at your kitchen sink, you are the common denominator who determines if you appear as the leading lady or supporting character.

Are you among those women hiding their gifts because they believe they are just ordinary instead of uniquely extraordinary?

What if you had an impact on someone else's life because you shared your gifts? Those unexpected gifts that leave us breathless, startled, and confused.

Those unexpected gifts that show up while you were busy coping with life's everyday challenges. Losing a job or a cancer diagnosis and figuring out your next best move. Whether it is the death of a loved one or the end of a life you thought you could depend on, you are resilient and found a way to move forward. You are a solution identifier, a compassionate listener, and a magician who can transform a mishap into a marvelous discovery.

I invite you to give yourself permission to claim your starring role in your story of challenges becoming unexpected gifts. Share with the world about those times where you were in the right place at the right time so that you could step into being your own hero. It's time for you to shine in your brilliance.

—Daily inspiration by Mary E. Knippel, Writer Unleashed

11.

Forgiveness and Thankfulness

The wise understand the need to avoid stagnation and regression. **You can be thankful for all the experiences that you endure because they made you better, stronger, and wiser.** You are among the few privileged ones who have experienced the full cycle of life. **Forgiveness is your only path to freedom.** You must be grateful and forgive yourself and others. You remain chained to those who offended you, and they still have some power over you until you forgive them. By forgiving, you set yourself free to move forward.

The Golden Rule asks us to treat others as we would like to be treated. It means we must forgive others first if we want them to forgive us; we must offer the best of what we have first to others if we want them to give us their best. **What you have learned through the ups and downs of life is precious. Select the best and prepare to share it with others, just as the farmer keeps the best seeds for his next season.** What are you thankful for? What wisdom or insight are you sharing with those around you?

—*Daily inspiration by Fabien W. Edjou, Author & Life Coach*

12.

Thought for the Day

"Do you want to meet the love of your life? Look in the mirror."

—BYRON KATIE

13.

Accept the Gift of You

"Promise me; you will always remember: You're braver than you believe and stronger than you seem, and smarter than you think."

—CHRISTOPHER ROBIN TO WINNIE
THE POOH, AS WRITTEN BY A.A. MILNE

If you were to ask your friends or family what your strengths are—or begin to notice more of the nice things others say about you—would you take in and accept those beautiful sentiments about yourself?

Many of us would not because we were taught to be modest, not to brag, and not to call attention to ourselves. So, we can look at those nice things as biased or not objective facts about us.

And we reject them.

Here's a truth: If they perceive positive things about you, then in their world, it is true for them and therefore, can be true for you, too.

Receive it graciously! Own it! Love it! Be empowered by all the wonderful aspects of yourself so you can shine those gifts in the world. **We need you to shine and inspire us to shine also.**

All of us have those days when we aren't feeling so grateful for ourselves. It's not good to travel down that spiral for too long. **It's time for some emergency self-care.**

Exercise. Movement and exercise release endorphins to pick up your spirits. It helps you get clearer about those negative thoughts you're having, so you can shift those falsehoods into truth.

Journal on something positive about yourself. Release those feel-good chemicals, oxytocin, serotonin, and dopamine in your brain by thinking of something positive.

Meditate or pray. Stop, breathe, go within. Focus on past achievements because this allows the brain to relive the experience as if it is currently happening.

—Daily inspiration by Dr. Kimberly Schehrer, Teen Breakthrough Expert

14.

Thought for the Day

"What you do has far greater impact than what you say."

—STEPHEN COVEY

15.

Gratitude

"Wear gratitude like a cloak, and it will feed every corner of your life."

—RUMI

As Thanksgiving approaches, we frequently are challenged to remember everything in your life for which you are grateful. Some years that is easy, and some years it is not. It is okay to have both types of years.

We need the lows in order to appreciate the highs. We need the darkness to appreciate the light.

Of course, you can always be grateful to be alive, to have feelings, and to live in a human body to move whenever your heart desires. For if you start with small gratitude, especially in the times when you feel there is nothing to be thankful for, look to find small improvement and meaningful moments. They count too. If we look closely enough and with openness, we can always find something to be thankful for. Small steps and improvements count too.

—Daily inspiration by Dr. Sarah Breen

16.

November Tribute

Solemn moments paid to tribute those who came before us. Those who bravely stood in damp and muddy trenches, to outlast those who would destroy us.

In November, we give thanks for the feast we're about to receive. We celebrate the bounty and join in the generosity. I am grateful for my freedom to express. The words I write so liberally to get the lump off of my chest. I am grateful for all my liberties. Many lost their lives so that I could build these memories.

In November, I am inspired by the greatest generation. The ones who offered so much when all they had was so much less.

In November, I am grateful for all of my abilities. I will remind myself to use them to be the best that I can be. **And as my kindest tribute, I give those around me my very best.**

To what are you giving tribute? For what are you thankful? How can you share your gifts, talents, and abilities to lift up others?

—Daily inspiration by Leigh Bursey, Musician, Speaker, and Municipal Councillor

17.

Thought for the Day

"Your need for acceptance can make you invisible in this world. Don't let anything stand in the way of the light that shines through this form. Risk being seen in all of your glory."

—JIM CARREY

18.

Thought for the Day

"Reflect upon your present blessings—of which every man has many—not on your past misfortunes, of which all men have some."

—CHARLES DICKENS

19.

It is a Courageous Act to Say "Yes" to *You*

From a childhood of abuse, I know a lot about being disempowered and how to overcome that in order to step into my passion, power, and gifts. The gift I have found is my passion for helping other women step forward and into their courageous and empowered selves, no matter what.

Today I celebrate you for saying "yes" to your journey. I know you have your own stories or messages you have received that have disempowered you in some way. I also know that you are taking the journey to stand up, focus on your purpose and joy, and **shine**!

I encourage you not to take this journey alone. **It is also a courageous act to be willing to let others walk beside you** to support and cheer you on in life. I invite you to pause, take a deep breath, and be ready to receive the inspiration and wisdom of others who are on this journey with you. We need others to encourage us, to speak wisdom and truth into us, to love us and cheer us on, and to help us stand up again when we fall. And to help us stay courageous and continue to say "yes" to ourselves.

Take that in, along with the magical, beautiful warmth of a June day.

—**Daily inspiration by Rebecca Hall Gruyter, Influencer and Empowerment Leader**

20.

Enough

You've got this.

Always remember you are enough.

—Daily inspiration Maureen Ryan Blake, Founder and Principal of The Power of the Tribe

21.

Forgiveness

We all have little spats or large fights with family and friends. The way we get past them is through forgiveness.

This came hard for me since my first husband left me in 1992. It was so bad that when I prayed the Lord's Prayer during prayer groups, when we got to the words, "and forgive those who trespass against us," I couldn't even say the words.

During one of these groups, a spiritual visitor guided me through forgiveness and explained it's not forgiving the other person for what they did. It's forgiving ourselves for allowing it to affect our lives.

This was a strong awakening. My biggest hurt was when my first husband left my three young children and me. It devastated me, and I couldn't let it go for many years.

Once I learned about forgiveness, it was like a weight was lifted. I could move forward, find joy, and be thankful again.

When we celebrate Thanksgiving, I am always thankful for this great lesson. What are you thankful for this season?

—Daily inspiration by Catherine M. Laub, Podcast Host

22.

Are You Hiding Your Light?

*"The only one keeping us a best-kept secret is ourselves,
and the only one who can share it is ourselves."*

—REBECCA HALL GRUYTER

When I talk to people about their business and their message, so many of them tell me that they want to make a positive difference. I notice that while they truly want to make a powerful difference in the world, many don't know how to go about making that happen. These beautiful, generous, gifted people are the best-kept secret, defined as *something very good that not many people know about*. They are hiding their light that they could be *shining* out into the world.

Perhaps you, too, want to make a positive difference, to impact people in a powerful, transformative way. **Do people know that about you? Do they know how to find you? Are you hiding your light?**

I have discovered that if the people who need you cannot see you and hear you, then you cannot help them. This is why I believe visibility is so important. Visibility is about being seen in such a way that you are easy for people to find.

Too many of us are waiting on the sidelines to be discovered! But the truth is: No one can make your dreams come true except you—your positive impact is not going to happen by keeping it a secret. **If you want to make a difference, you have to lead your own effort.** Become a spokesperson for your message, your product launch, your book, standing for what you believe and bringing that forward rather than merely hoping it will speak for itself. If your visibility is low, then it's up to you to raise it—no one else can do it better than you can!

—Daily inspiration by Rebecca Hall Gruyter, Influencer and Empowerment Leader

23.

Focus

*"Your strongest muscle and worst enemy
is your mind. Train it well."*

—LISE GOTTLEIB

"We can control our lives by controlling our perceptions."

—BRUCE LIPTON, THE BIOLOGY OF BELIEF

Our minds are hardwired to look for the negative in our experience in order to prevent the things we don't want from coming into our lives. This is our animal instinct at play. The problem is that only looking out for the unwanted experiences actually puts those experiences into your mind, and you begin to see them more and more. In order to change what you are focusing on, you must do it consciously and with intention. Seemingly good things, just as often as things you perceive as bad, are happening simultaneously. The problem is what you are focusing on.

Each day set your intention to focus on the things for which you are grateful. It can be as seemingly inconsequential as a warm beverage in the morning, the sound of the wind and rain, the feeling of the air blowing through your hair. What you focus on will grow. This practice of training your attention to look for the positive has to be done in the morning to prepare you for your day, and at night, so you can relax into a peaceful sleep. This practice will help you actually focus on what you want more of in your life. Be present and savor each moment.

—Daily inspiration by Kimi Avary, MA, Relationship Navigation Specialist

24.

Thought for the Day

"A lot of people are afraid to say what they want. That's why they don't get what they want."

—MADONNA

25.

Thought for the Day

"Turn your wounds into wisdom."

—OPRAH WINFREY

26.

Stop, Pause, and Be Still

One vacation I will always remember was the school trip to Europe with my daughter. It was a beautiful Saturday morning; after a wonderful time spent in Germany with tours of castles and museums, we boarded our private coach headed for Italy. It was quiet and serene as the bus traveled through the Alps as students and staff reflected on their past few days and anticipated the upcoming ones. As the bus ambled through the mountains, with music softly playing, as far as the eye could see, from the valley below to the tallest peak of the Alps, snow was falling from the heavens in all its beauty and glistening grandeur.

Suddenly, with such a melodious tone, as if the angels were playing their harps, "How Great Thou Art" began to play. As we looked at the spectacular white beauty of nature, the majestic feel of the high heavens, each one in their own thoughts, we experienced love, peace, and calmness that only comes from above, and we knew that God cared. **That morning, we learned what it means to experience total gratitude, beauty, peace, and praise to the Creator.**

Today, stop, pause, and appreciate the beauty and grandeur around you. Be still for a moment and give thanks for this moment of beauty and peace.

—*Daily inspiration by Toni Stone Bruce, Precious Stones 4 Life, LLC*

27.

Thought for the Day

"If you're offered a seat on a rocket ship, don't ask what seat! Just get on."

—SHERYL SANDBERG

28.

Stop. Breathe. Check-in.

Do you ever have periods in your work or business where it feels like a blur, when things just keep moving at a speeding pace, and you never quite get control of things or have a handle on what just happened?

In these times, our heads are full, stress-producing hormones are rising, time seems to fly, and we forget ourselves. We forget to breathe, to be present, to be mindful of the wonderful gift that we are. Here are some ways that I have learned and shared with others to be more present in every precious moment of life.

Stop and remember why you are here. You are here on purpose, and you have a purpose for everything you do—right at this moment, and this one, and this one.

Remind yourself of who you are and how wonderful you are. How beautiful and unique you are and how you show up in the world.

Be present to your experience. Before you start an activity or attend an event, or even just starting your day, take some moments to ask yourself: "What is it that I need to know or to have today? What is it that will encourage me, equip me, empower me to bring in my magic [in this activity]?"

There's real power in stopping and checking in with yourself. It helps keep you grounded and clear, no matter what. **Remember to stop, pause, and breathe.**

—*Daily inspiration by Rebecca Hall Gruyter, Influencer and Empowerment Leader*

29.

Thought for the Day

"Remember no one can make you feel inferior without your consent."

—ELEANOR ROOSEVELT

30.

Perspective

"Sometimes, you have to take a step back to look at your situation from a different angle to find a different solution."

—DR. GREG REID

Perspective is everything. How we see the world is how we interpret what we see. When we change our space, our angle, our vantage point, we can see what is already there but with fresh eyes, seeing what we might not have seen before. Think of a dance floor. We have one view on the dance floor. The view changes if we are in the next level up in the balcony or the mezzanine. Were we wrong before? No. Our view was simply different, perhaps incomplete, as we only saw from our point of view at that moment in time. When we consider a stakeholder approach—we look through the lens of *all* stakeholders to see the world as they see it. The view is different from the top of the mountain than from the foothills. How we see the problem is often how we see its solution. **Can't see the solution from where you are? Try a different view, a different height, a different perspective.** Inspiration can simply be a shift in perspective and only a step away.

—*Daily inspiration by Dr. Cheryl Lentz, The Academic Entrepreneur*

December

1.

A Time to Give

Christmas is my favorite season of the year. It's filled with excitement and color, holiday songs, and festivity. The house is smelling delicious as candied yams, macaroni and cheese, pies, and cakes are being baked. The Christmas tree is put up and decorated by family members laughing and sharing stories. There's love in the air for family and quiet dedication to baby Jesus, thankful for His birth.

As we share this holiday season with family and friends, enjoying each moment, let's remember those who are less fortunate than us. This is a perfect time to share your gifts and monies to organizations and families in need. This is a good time in your giving to share with a charity that no one may consider. I had the privilege of being the mistress of ceremony for a fundraiser for the Conklin Center for the Blind. I experienced such joy as I talked to the residents and heard their stories. They are individuals just like us, experiencing more challenges, yet with determination to find their place in life. My mom lost her sight due to a brain tumor for fifteen years, yet I learned so much from her.

This season, give our time and monies to a charity and be a blessing. "Oh, come all ye faithful, joyful, and triumphant." Just have faith and do it! Be blessed!

—Daily inspiration by Toni Stone Bruce, Precious Stones 4 Life, LLC

2.

Wonder in Your Life

How special is the wonderment of children—when we don't have any fear and treat all beings the same way, without judgment!

In what ways do you still see wondrous things in your life?

Even as an adult, I like to look for wonder in my life, to see the magic that might present itself to me at any moment. There is a powerful exercise to invite in wonderment and magic by setting your expectations for it.

When you are about to enter a new situation or go to an event, check-in with yourself by asking:

• *What is it that I need to know or have [in this situation or at this event]?*

• *What will encourage me, equip me, empower me to bring in my magic?*

• *What is it that I'm willing to receive in this experience I am about to have?*

Then, open yourself up to connect with the answers. You may find wonder in the most unexpected places!

We are empowered with the choice to hold things in our lives in wonder and awe. We can make decisions about what we will trust and how we will treat each other. We can choose the lens through which we see our world. I hope you choose to see the wonder, love, and magic in the world.

—Daily inspiration by Rebecca Hall Gruyter, Influencer and Empowerment Leader

3.

Thought for the Day

"The stars shine a little brighter when I tell them about you."

—SIRAPA MALLA

4.

Beautiful Enough

Between Black Friday and about mid-February, Christmas decorations surround my house.

When my kids lived at home, we had a large tree and lots of presents. When they moved out, we set up a four-foot tree. My biggest decorating was creating many ceramic house villages throughout the house. Tony, my husband, lived to ski, so there was a ski village along with a fishing town for his love of boats.

Christmas 2019 was different. Tony was dying, so we didn't plan to celebrate the holidays. I discovered it was important to still decide to celebrate and continue with life even with all we were facing. I did put up our tree and bought a handful of angels to place on it.

My "village" covered a small table, with tiny houses, and little stuffed snowmen I acquired that same year when my mother died, plus a few reindeer. (We chose the most meaningful parts for us to celebrate with. This lifted us up.) Tony said it was beautiful and enough.

Although Tony is gone, I will continue to love Christmas and decorate with smaller houses and villages. I now know there is such a thing as "beautiful enough," and it is important to remember to bring forward our special traditions, especially during challenging times. Christmas will continue to be my favorite holiday, and I'm finding new joys and ways to celebrate.

What do you do to brighten the season for you and your family?

—Daily inspiration by Catherine M. Laub, Podcast Host

5.

Thought for the Day

"Our hearts grow tender with childhood memories and love of kindred, and we are better throughout the year for having, in spirit, become a child again at Christmas-time."

—LAURA INGALLS WILDER

6.

Thought for the Day

"Let all your thinks be thanks."

—W.H. AUDEN

7.

The Joy of Giving

"No one is useless in this world who lightens the burdens of another."

—CHARLES DICKENS

We are all connected—teens, parents, friends, families, old people and babies, in our neighborhood and all around the world. What keeps us connected, and what many of us practice, especially this month, are *kindness and generosity*. As we give and receive gifts, it's a great opportunity to teach the children and teens in your life about the joy of giving.

Here are some ways that you and your young loved ones can practice the joy of giving.

For family and friends:

Acknowledge someone for a quality you appreciate about them.

Spend time with them by listening or giving encouragement.

Do a kind act without being asked, such as cooking dinner or emptying the dishwasher.

For the community:

Smile at a stranger.

Look for a volunteer project you can take part in with a team or committee.

Reach out to a new student to include them.

For the world:

Donate to a cause you care about or post a fundraising activity on your social media.

Begin a thirty-day challenge to show an act of kindness each day and ask that each person post their daily acts of kindness. This will have a ripple effect.

Email gratitude for service to a veteran's organization or first responders in another part of the world.

These kinds of activities will show your loved ones that the joy of giving enhances the miracles that show up in their life!

—*Daily inspiration by Dr. Kimberly Schehrer, Teen Breakthrough Expert*

8.

Thought for the Day

*"It's not how much we give but
how much love we put into giving."*

—MOTHER THERESA

9.

Feed Your Soul

The end of the year is here. There are so many celebrations that occur in this month. A look back at the past and a look ahead to the future. **Surround yourself with those who feed your soul.** As children, we care most about the gifts and the parties. As adults, we seek a deeper meaning to these holidays. Some find them solely religious and some not at all.

All of us, though, can agree that throughout this time of year, what we truly crave are the bonds with family and friends. Find those people that make you feel on the inside what the gifts used to make you feel like a child—the people that light you up. That is where you are supposed to be now and forever.

—Daily inspiration by Dr. Sarah Breen

10.

Thought for the Day

"Never dull your shine for somebody else."

—TYRA BANKS

11.

Beautiful Gifts

One year when the kids were younger, we were making plans for a family vacation along the shores of beautiful Lake Michigan. We had a budget. I worked hard to find a house that would suit our family but not break the bank. But I was late to start looking, so it was a bit of work to find one. But I finally did. The only drawback: it was right next to an active train track. *Right next* to the tracks. Literally.

The fine print assured me that the train only ran at 11 p.m. and 3 a.m. Well, that's good when you consider safety for the family. But, maybe not great for sleeping

—on vacation! It was too late to find something else. So, I held my breath and hoped that it would be manageable.

Can I just tell you that the train track actually became a great family memory? Our trick: pennies on the track! A few evenings that week, we snuck out late at night and placed our pennies along the track—sort of a pre-tuck-in routine. The next morning, still in PJs, the kids would rush out to find their flattened treasures. Somewhere else in Grand Haven, someone else was sleeping-in in a nicer house in a better location that they had probably secured earlier in the year. Meanwhile, the PJ-clad McKees were dancing in the morning light, finding freshly flattened pennies, and saving them like treasures from our time together.

Was it my plan? Nope. But sometimes our mistakes or delays can turn into beautiful gifts.

—*Daily inspiration by Shannon McKee, Author, Mentor, and Life Coach*

12.

Rebirth or Gift

"The person who screams the loudest on the point of death is the person who never lived at all."

—LEO BUSCAGLIA

The holidays are an interesting time. It's the intersection of lifelessness and festivities. The harvest is complete. The plants are empty, dying, and well into the dormancy phase of their lifecycle. Winter is in full swing. **It's time for shedding the old and no longer useful in preparation for rebirth.** It's also an opportunity to take stock and to consciously choose what to embrace and what to release in your life. Simultaneously, it's the time of celebrations, family gatherings, and making merry with friends. Often this time feels so busy that we can hardly breathe.

I invite you to make some appointments just for *you* in your hectic schedule to pause, listen to your soul, and think about what is truly important to you. Ask yourself, "If today was my last day, would I be happy with the life I've lived?" Listen to the answer. It's the essence of your soul's wisdom. Write down what your soul is saying. Write, just to write, and see what journey it takes you on. Are you on the path of a life well-lived, or are you off track? Do you need to course-correct? When you're done, look for the messages. They are like holiday gifts waiting to be unwrapped. The truth is that you just being you is a great gift to the world.

—Daily inspiration by Kimi Avary, MA, Relationship Navigation Specialist

13.

Thought for the Day

"The best and most beautiful things in this world cannot be seen or even heard, but must be felt with the heart."

—HELEN KELLER

14.

Your Tribe

*"When a woman loses her tribe, she loses her shine,
but when we come together, we shine brighter."*

—MAUREEN RYAN-BLAKE

Remember to spend time with your tribe. Recharge, connect, and *shine!*

—Daily inspiration by Maureen Ryan Blake, Founder and Principal of The Power of the Tribe

15.

Patches, The Christmas Cat

Is it possible for a little, black-and-white, spotted, furry, twelve-pound being to have an impact on every life he touched?

Yes! That was my Patches. There was something so special about Patches, who joined my life one Christmas as a kitten and stayed with me for seventeen years. He captivated hearts with his spirit, love of others, and powerful presence.

Even those who weren't "cat people" were drawn to him. He brought joy, love, and peace to all those around him. If a friend came to visit me upset over something, Patches would come to curl up next to them or lay on their lap. It was as if he understood that they needed some extra love in those moments.

People would call me all the time to share how Patches just understood them when they were having a really bad day. They would come and visit him. In fact, in his final days, people stopped by to spend time with him and thank him. They shared their love and presence with him just as he once had with them.

It's no surprise that the Christmas cat left a lasting legacy to me and all the lives and hearts he touched. I miss him but feel his heart and spirit every Christmas, and it makes me smile and feel loved.

Do you have a furry or feathered friend in your life who has left a beautiful legacy to your life? Celebrate the gift they have been and are in your life.

—*Daily inspiration by Rebecca Hall Gruyter, Influencer and Empowerment Leader*

16.

The Gift of You

I believe a knowledge not shared is worthless. You've gone through and mastered some facets of life. As a master, you understand nothing is static in life; there is no standstill; you either regress or progress. The path to your progress is through mentorship. The master sees himself anew through mentoring and transforming the apprentice. As a master, have a transformative power endowed to you. This power is magnetic and manifests externally as an attraction. **You are now considered a source of inspiration and wisdom.**

Give in abundance to many who want to be like you and are attracted to seek life advice. The best gift you can offer to the world cannot be purchased in any store. You give to the world by your way of being, how you carry yourself, how you treat others and the consistency between your words and actions. You don't need to waste energy to lecture others because they are observing you even in secret; they learn by watching, and they change by emulating. Shine and glow to a perennial circle of life and build a legacy. This is how you truly become the salt of the earth and the light of the world. Shine brightly for all to see!

—Daily inspiration by Fabien W. Edjou, Author & Life Coach

17.

Thought for the Day

"All our dreams can come true, if we
have the courage to pursue them."

—WALT DISNEY

18.

Thought for the Day

"I find that it's the simple things that remind you of family around the holidays."

—AMY ADAMS

19.

Choose to Share the Gift of You with the World

"Insanity: doing the same thing over and over again and expecting different results."

—UNKNOWN

The world is waiting for the gift of more of you! I know you are sharing what you're called forth to bring to the world in your life and business. And I encourage and support you to share even more of you!

Let's check in on how you're doing: What actions are you taking that you'll be practicing or implementing that are different from last year (further expanding and helping you grow) and will bring you different results that you want?

Often, we can be doing the same things—just pushing harder—and be expecting different results. You have choices in everything that you're doing and can make different choices that better serve you. Think about what you can choose to echo out, the things that will allow you to be seen and heard, even more, to be visible!

Visibility is how you are showing up in the world. It could be on stage, on the radio, or on the grocery line! I believe so much that **visibility is how you best share the gift of yourself with the world.**

Today, think about how you are showing up in your life for yourself and for others. **You are called to be visible, to show up exactly as you are made.** Be willing to build new practices and take new actions today that might be different from what you did last year so that you can be even more visible or in a different way that lets you *shine* even brighter.

—Daily inspiration by Rebecca Hall Gruyter, Influencer and Empowerment Leader

20.

Collective Kindness

As winter comes to greet us, and the daylight disappears, we surround ourselves with familiar symbols of holiday warmth, faith, mythology, and song.

For some, this is their peak performance—wrapping gifts and stapling twinkling lights to their shingled rooftops. For many, this is the hardest period to exist in a world filled with celebratory mantras. It's a time when many are confronted with loss, regret, and emptiness.

That is why our collective kindness is so paramount in times of sorrow.

In December, I am grateful that I grew up poor.

I am grateful that the warmth and love of a teenage mother helped me to appreciate the moments when love was enough and when enjoying the colorful lights of neighborhood homes was more than enough to make up for not having our own.

In December, I am grateful for the warm meals and hot chocolate, and for her many overtime hours worked on holidays so that I could get that special Batman action figure, even if it meant she was hardly there to see me pose him as the victor who finally vanquishes the Joker atop the imaginary skyscraper in my mind.

In December, I draw inspiration from a mother's love and the lessons learned through modesty.

In December, I am reminded of how Ebenezer Scrooge finally has his moment of clarity.

How wealth, like kindness, is better when it's shared. Let's take a moment today to share kindness and love with each other.

—*Daily inspiration by Leigh Bursey, Musician, Speaker, and Municipal Councillor*

21.

Thought for the Day

"If you can tune into your purpose and really align with it, setting goals so that your vision is an expression of that purpose, then life flows much more easily."

—JACK CANFIELD

22.

Thought for the Day

"May your walls know joy, may every room hold laughter, and every window open to great possibility"

—MARY ANNE RADMACHER

23.

Be Willing to Share

Share Confidently and Be Open to Others

Everyone has a story worth sharing. I wrote a book recently that deeply impacted readers. I've been called a role model. I've been called a leader. I don't feel like one.

My story is not more compelling or more tragic or more uplifting than the stories of others. There was one key thing that put me in front of others. I was willing to tell my story, even parts I was scared to share. It isn't that I am wiser or more experienced than others. My story is as unique as anyone else's, but also no more unique. It is one story in billions, and this isn't a competition. This isn't about who has the best story. It is about us collectively banding together and helping one another thrive.

We need repetition. We need reminders. We need reinforcement. We forget. We all need to listen to the stories of others. They will remind and reinforce the important lessons we have learned along the way.

Share openly with others. Your story has value. Others will benefit from hearing it. They will be reminded. Lessons and beliefs will be reinforced. You don't need to win any competitions or prizes, but we will all benefit from your willingness and your courage, as you will from others. Be willing to share your story.

—Daily inspiration by Patrick P. Long, International Best-Selling Author

24.

Clear Direction

"If you don't know where you're going, any path will do."

—THE CHESHIRE CAT, ALICE IN WONDERLAND

This question that many struggle with is not new. "Which way should I go?" often brings us to a crossroads many times in our life. **The challenge is if we don't have a direction, how do we know which choice to make?**

I have absolutely *no* sense of geographic direction. Absolutely none—just not in my wheelhouse. Because of this, I always leave the house with my Ask Google Directions App, with a GPS unit in the car, and written directions as a backup, particularly on a rainy day. Why? Getting lost is frustrating, and I hate being late. So, I know exactly where I'm going and how to get there before I *ever* leave the house.

The principle is the same here. **Know the destination.** This way, you are assured of getting there. Now, *how* is a whole different conversation, as sometimes our journey can be different than we expect. However, the universe can only take us where we ask and want to go if we provide the address—the goal, the endpoint. Review SMART goals—**S**pecific, **M**easurable, **A**ttainable, **R**ealistic, and **T**imely. Know before you go. Yes, there are sometimes detours and potholes along the way; however, follow the cat. If we don't know *where*, life won't take us there.

—*Daily inspiration by Dr. Cheryl Lentz, The Academic Entrepreneur*

25.

Thought for the Day

*"Don't let the past steal your present. This is the
message of Christmas: We are never alone."*

—TAYLOR CALDWELL

26.

Aim for the Sky in the New Year!

"It's not that we aim too high and miss, it's that we aim too low and hit."
-Les Brown

Let's explore how you will shine in the new year. This is the perfect time to look at your future—where are you going, what are you called to be, and where are you called to stretch. **I encourage you to aim high and far, aim further than you can even see exactly where it will land!**

Set goals for yourself that scare you a little bit, aren't the safe route, or are somewhere you have never been before. You don't have to know the *how*; you can figure that out later. **Look for opportunities to reach for that thing that's so far out there you can hardly believe you're claiming it.** A goal that, if you told people, they wouldn't even know how you are going to reach. You feel a quickening in your spirit and a little bit of terror, but you're going to do it anyway—the sky's the limit!

When we're bringing magic into your life and into others' lives, it takes a willingness to set those goals, a willingness to go where we haven't gone before, to stand out, to *shine*! Aim high!

—Daily inspiration by Rebecca Hall Gruyter, Influencer and Empowerment Leader

27.

Winter "Bless"

One of the best gifts we can give this holiday season is helping our family, friends, colleagues, and clients bloom and *shine* in the new year. But before we can share our blessings with others, we need to have something to *give*.

During a challenging season in my life one winter, I was so emotionally spent, **I felt like I had nothing left to give.** That's when I discovered a simple, yet profound cure, and I'm happy to share with you today. **During this beautiful season of giving, here's a special tip on how to also bless yourself: Take time away from others and spend quiet time with God.** Block out time in your calendar (and **keep this appointment with yourself**!). Decide which activity to choose that will best serve your spiritual quiet time during this busy holiday season. Will you meditate? Journal? Nature walk? Crochet? Create? Play inspirational holiday music? Dance? Cook? Or simply *be still* and listen? These activities only take five minutes to one hour of your time, depending on which activity you do, but the health rewards from this spiritual self-care are priceless. The beautiful benefits you can expect to receive include a refreshed state of mind a renewed spirit, a reconnection to your truth, and restoration of **peace and joy.** There's no better time than now to soak in bubbles, celebrate with bubbles, bloom and *shine*! With bright blessings this holiday season and in the new year from my home to yours!

—*Daily inspiration by Marlene Elizabeth, author of Moneywings™*

28.

Thought for the Day

*"There are far better things ahead
than any we leave behind."*

—C.S. LEWIS

29.

Thought for the Day

"Happiness is there for the taking, and the making."

—OPRAH WINFREY

30.

Heart Anniversary

"The secret anniversaries of the heart..."

—HENRY WADSWORTH LONGFELLOW

Today I invite you to consider holding sacred the present moment with as much reverence as you do for whatever took place yesterday or yesteryear.

What comes to mind when you think of holidays and secret anniversaries of the heart? Special milestone birthdays? The day you graduated from high school/college? Where you were standing when you got your first kiss? The last time you talked to someone you love? What you did to get ready for your first day on the job? These are all cherished memories and deserve to be honored.

When I was growing up, holidays were a big deal. We had a parade on Memorial Day where the American Legion honor guard marched down Main Street to the cemetery and where they fired off a twenty-one-gun salute. We had a Fourth of July parade with floats, a marching band, sparklers, and fireworks.

Later, the children lined up the Saturday before Christmas at the furniture store to talk to Santa seated on his La-Z-Boy throne.

Give yourself permission to pause right now and take a breath when you feel yourself getting too caught up in damage control over yesterday's blunder or prepping for tomorrow's undertaking.

Savor the opportunity to be in the present moment in the here and now. Just be and choose to take joy in your life as it unfolds minute by minute, hour by hour, one heartbeat at a time.

—Daily inspiration by Mary E. Knippel, Writer Unleashed

31.

Thought for the Day

"Tomorrow is the first blank page of a 365-page book. Write a good one."

—BRAD PAISLEY

A NOTE FROM REBECCA

Dear Powerful Reader,,

Thank you for reading our anthology. I hope it has touched your heart and spirit, encouraging and inspiring you!

I wanted to share a little bit more about our organizations, Your Purpose Driven Practice™ and RHG Media Productions™. We are passionate about helping others live on purpose and with purpose in their life and business. I hope this book has supported and inspired you to choose to live on purpose and with great purpose!

If you are wanting to reach more people and be part of inspiring and supporting others with your message, your gifts, and the work that you bring to the world, then I want to share some opportunities for you to consider.

Each year, we compile and produce anthology book projects, support authors in publishing their own powerful books as best sellers, produce and publish an international magazine, launch TV shows, facilitate women's empowerment conferences, launch radio and podcast shows, and help experts and speakers step into a place of powerful influence to make a global difference. We provide programs and strategies to help you reach more people and facilitate the Speaker Talent Search (which helps speakers, experts, and influencers connect with more speaking opportunities). We would love to support you in reaching more people. Please take a moment to learn a little bit more about us at the sites listed below, and then reach out to us for a conversation. **We would love to have you join us as we seek to make a positive global difference.**

You can learn more about each of these things are our main website: www.YourPurposeDrivenPractice.com

Enjoy our powerful **TV and podcast shows**: www.RHGTVNetwork.com

Learn more about the **Speaker Talent Search™:**

www.SpeakerTalentSearch.com

Join Rebecca's pool of experts for hosts looking for great talent to interview on their shows called **RHG Expert Connections**:

www.RHGExpertConnections.com

Learn more about our **anthology writing opportunities**:

www.YourPurposeDrivenPractice.com and click on the "anthology writing opportunities" button.

If you would like to connect with me personally to explore some of our opportunities in upcoming book projects, podcast/radio shows, and/or TV, here is the link to schedule a time to speak with me directly: www.MeetWithRebecca.com, or you can email me at Rebecca@YourPuposeDrivenPractice.com

May you always choose to step forward and SHINE!

Warmly,

Rebecca Hall Gruyter

BY SUBJECT

Bloom/Grow
January: 4, 9, 10, 13, 21
February: 2, 20
March: 13, 17, 19
April: 2, 5, 8, 14, 30
May: 5
June: 2, 18, 28
July: 24
August: 18
September: 1, 4, 12
October: 3, 11

Change:
January: 8
March: 5, 8
April: 2, 20
July: 15, 28, 31
August: 25
September: 30

Choice
January: 3, 4, 14, 20, 27
February: 1, 7)
March: 8, 9, 11, 24, 27
April: 1, 5, 29
May: 5, 6, 12, 15, 18, 22, 29, 30
June: 12, 15, 17, 22, 23, 24, 29
July: 3, 6, 12, 14, 21, 29
August: 3, 9, 15, 18, 23, 30, 31
September: 2, 6, 11, 17, 18, 21, 23, 26
October: 7, 15, 21, 31
November: 3, 4, 6, 7, 10, 14, 19, 24, 27, 28
December: 2, 9, 12, 23, 24, 31

Encouragement/Inspiration/Hope
January: 1, 8
February: 3, 4, 18
March: 4, 19, 24, 26
April: 15, 21
May: 20, 31
June: 2, 15, 25
July: 16, 24
August: 9, 21
September: 1, 26
October: 1, 7, 8
November: 3, 19, 20
December: 3, 7, 27, 28

Faith/Trust
January: 15, 28
February: 24
March: 4
April: 8
July: 14
August: 5, 13
October: 11

Family/Relationships
February: 6, 13
March: 30
April: 2, 9, 11, 27
May: 3, 11, 13, 16, 23
June: 6, 20
July: 1, 5, 9, 13, 18, 29
August: 7
September: 5, 6
October: 15, 29

Family/Relationships (Cont.)
November: 2
December: 4, 7, 11, 18

Fear/Failure/
Overcoming/Courage
January: 3, 15, 16, 19, 25, 26, 27
February: 1, 10, 21, 25, 28
March: 2, 3, 5, 7, 10
April: 19, 22, 28
May: 8, 9, 14, 19, 22, 26
June: 7, 11, 16, 19, 27
July: 23, 25
August: 2, 4, 9, 17, 19, 29, 31
September: 16, 20
October: 2, 3, 6, 9, 10, 19, 20, 24, 25, 28, 30
November: 8, 19, 21, 23, 25
December: 17

Gratitude/Celebration
January: 14
February: 9
March: 5
May: 21
June: 9
July: 4, 8, 10, 11, 30
August: 16, 27
September: 14
October: 13, 23
November: 1, 2, 5, 6, 8, 9, 11, 15, 16, 18, 21, 23
December: 1, 6, 7, 9, 11, 20

Holiday/Seasons
January: 10, 21
March: 2, 19
April: 16
May: 3, 16, 23
June: 4, 6, 24
July: 8, 30
August: 6, 12, 27
September: 28
October: 13, 23
November: 16
December: 15, 20, 25, 30, 31

Joy/Peace/Happiness
February: 13
March: 14, 15, 16
April: 26
May: 6, 24
June: 4
August: 22
September: 15, 24
October: 4, 18
December: 22, 27, 29

Loss/Grief
February: 16, 18
March: 17

Love:
January: 17, 29
February: 3, 6, 8, 9, 11, 12, 13, 17, 27
March: 28
April: 12, 17, 23
June: 20
July: 9, 17
September: 19
October: 29
November: 12
December: 8, 20

Mindset/Perspective
January: 8, 14, 20
February: 1, 4, 7, 12
March: 13, 21, 26
May: 6, 12, 28
June: 8, 27
October: 15, 17
November: 23, 30
December: 2, 11, 13, 24

Money
March: 11
May: 28
August: 8
October: 14
December: 1

LEARN MORE ABOUT
OUR AUTHORS

Catherine M. Laub, Your Turquoise Angel Guide, is the host of The Celestial Spoon Radio Podcast, an 18-time award-winning inspirational author, an advocate for suicide prevention, and a psychic and spiritual Guide. Catherine helps people feel better with her positive outlook and describing overcoming her own deep depression. She is an advocate for mental illness through her campaign "Brighten Your Day with Turquoise." Turquoise is a calming color and helps us think clearly. Her goal is to help others achieve their potential without all the obstacles that get in the way. She's had many health challenges and wants to guide others to understand how to live with illness and still have a normal life. She guides others through her spiritual skills to feel invigorated and empowered to go forward in their own struggles.

Catherine also psychically delivers information to people from the spiritual realm; their guides and angels benefit greatly from their lives. Catherine is a workshop facilitator and does readings at local events, as well as performing sessions with clients worldwide via phone and Skype, email, and in-person.

Her favorite pastimes are doing jigsaw puzzles and playing with her young grandchildren. She also loves to travel for vacation and business. Overall, she strives to be an inspiration to all and to make the world a better place through her love for others.

Remember to have faith and know you can pull through almost anything!

Email: catherine@catherinemlaub.com
Phone: 631-619-2040
Website: https://www.catherinemlaub.com/
Facebook:
https://www.facebook.com/catherine.laub.54
https://www.facebook.com/TheCelestialSpoon
https://www.facebook.com/catherinemlaub.author/
LinkedIn: https://www.linkedin.com/in/catherinemlaub
Twitter: @cathysquests
YouTube: https://bit.ly/3f5DxNS
Other Social Media Channels:
The Celestial Spoon Podcast: https://apple.co/2SgQGty
Skype: cathyml58
Ezine Articles: https://bit.ly/3f3mj3E

Known as the *Academic Entrepreneur*, **Dr. Cheryl Lentz** is a unique speaker who intensely connects with her audience, having one foot in academia and one foot in the business and entrepreneurial space. Her goal is to offer the audience pearls of wisdom today that they can use tomorrow in their personal and professional lives. It is not enough to know; the expectation is for participants to take action and do. Join Dr. Cheryl on her journey to connect these dots to provide inspiration, knowledge, and counsel to move forward effectively.

Known globally for her writings on leadership and failure as well as critical and refractive thinking, she has been published more than 44 times with 25 writing awards. As an accomplished university professor, speaker, and consultant, she is an international best-selling author and top-quoted publishing professional on ABC, CBS, NBC, and Fox. She will take the stage as a TEDx Speaker for Farmingdale 2020 on October 10, 2020.

https://twitter.com/DrCherylLentz
https://www.amazon.com/Cheryl-Lentz/e/B002D63EPC
https://www.facebook.com/Dr.Cheryl.Lentz
email: drcheryllentz@gmail.com
https://www.linkedin.com/in/drcheryllentz/
https://www.youtube.com/drcheryllentz
https://www.instagram.com/drcheryllentz/

Fabien W. Edjou was born in Cameroon, Africa, and raised by a single mother. He started living alone and away from any family member at the early age of thirteen. He is a highly decorated, retired US Army officer. He was deployed three times and is a Purple Heart recipient who served as Senior HR Officer for the 97th Training Brigade CGSOC. Despite going through several existential life struggles such as business disappointments, friends' abandonment, a divorce, staggering debts, homelessness, loss of home, and custody of his children, he has never stopped being happy. In the midst of his own life struggles, he found his voice, and his desire to help others find meaning, purpose, and happiness grew even stronger. His message is simple: **"Happiness flows from inside out; therefore, anyone can access it anytime regardless of their life circumstances—rich, poor, young, old, or anything in between. You are the architect of your life and the master of your destiny."** He is a former host of "Revelations and Wonders: Secrets to Life and Happiness" talk show at Voice America World Radio. He has devoted his retirement from the military to spreading a message of hope and happiness. With a unique way of removing any perceived complexity in life, he explains with incredible simplicity and clarity the causes of our daily struggles and the way to address them. His audience considers him **"The best human being I've ever met,"** and a **"true beacon of light"** who **"will bring great joy to the world!"**

Email: fabienov@gmail.com
Phone: (952) 210-6068
Website: https://www.revelationsandwonders.com
Facebook:
https://www.facebook.com/fabien.edjou.7
https://www.facebook.com/RevelationsandWonders/
Twitter: @EdjouW
https://twitter.com/EdjouW
YouTube:
https://www.youtube.com/c/FabienEdjou
Other Social Media Channels:
https://www.linkedin.com/in/fabien-edjou-373bb641/
https://www.instagram.com/revelationsandwonders/
https://www.pinterest.com/fabienedjou/
https://www.linkedin.com/groups/13744798/
https://www.reddit.com/user/revelatnsandwonders
https://www.patreon.com/revelationsandwonders

Dr. Kimberly Schehrer is a Teen Breakthrough Expert and founder of Academy for Independence. She specializes in leadership, education, and personal development. She works closely with teens, who she feels are a misunderstood group brimming with potential. Dr. Kimberly has over 20 years of experience working with parents and teens as a Teen Breakthrough Expert, counselor, and an education specialist at schools, private institutions, and within the community in Silicon Valley and beyond. She is passionate about the next generation of leaders.

Dr. Kimberly's desire is for our teens to harness their greatest Superpower, themselves, just as they are, and up-level to unleash their full potential. Her passion is further ignited by watching them soar in the world to create transformation within themselves and their community. She nurtures our teens to lead their own lives according to their values, so they stand in their voice and confidently achieve their dreams with an unstoppable mindset. She is honored to have been cited in major media. Kimberly is a podcast host of the show Raising Unstoppable Teens and a #1 international best-selling author. Her recently released book, Unstoppable Teens: A Parent and Teen Guide to Teen Empowerment, Fulfillment and Achievement, and her journals are available on Amazon.

https://www.amazon.com/s?i=stripbooks&rh=p_27%3ADr.+Kimberly+Schehrer

Dr. Kimberly guided two daughters into thriving adulthood and lives in California with her fiancé, Robert, her beloved cat, Alice, and her faithful pup, Summer. She is passionate about the next generation of leaders and inspiring them to become unstoppable!

Email: Kimberly@afi4me.com
Phone: (831) 239-2788
Website: www.afi4me.com
FB: https://www.facebook.com/academyforindependence/
https://www.facebook.com/groups/
RaisingUnstoppableTeenswithDrKimberlySchehrer/
LI: https://www.linkedin.com/in/teen-breakthrough-expert/
IG: https://www.instagram.com/dr.kimberlyphd/
YouTube: https://youtube.com/user/Academy4Independence

Kimi Avary is an international speaker, author, and relationship coach. For over 15 years, she has helped men and women, singles and couples, overcome relationship challenges and open their hearts to love. She has a Master's in Counseling, is a Neuro-Linguistic Programming (NLP) Master Practitioner and trainer, and a Certified Relationship Coach through the Relationship Coaching Institute. She recently shared the stage with Caroline Myss and presidential candidate Marianne Williamson. Her upcoming book, Relationship Navigation: It Takes More Than Love, has been endorsed by Dr. John Gray of the Mars/Venus series. She is the creator of the Partnership Bliss Podcast and president of the Heart2Heart Toastmasters Club.

KimiAvary@gmail.com
650-714-4993
ConsciousCouplesNetwork.com
SymbolicGriefRitual.com
KimiAvary.com
Facebook.com/Kimi.Avary
Twitter.com/KimiAvary
Instagram.com/PartnershipBliss
Youtube.com/ConsciousCouplesNet

Leigh Bursey is a thirty-three-year-old, three-term municipal politician in Brockville, Ontario, Canada. He is also a record producer, singer-songwriter, and recording artist. He is a published poet, children's author, rock music journalist, and editorialist. He is a cable access television talk show host, hosting his program, *Critical Thinking*.

Leigh has acted in feature films and on network television shows. Leigh has modeled, performed as an amateur drag queen, and even dabbled in professional wrestling. His colorful life has seen him participate in dancing competitions, cage matches and battle royales, motivational speaking, and political campaigns, both foreign and domestic.

Leigh is also a survivor of addictions and cyclical poverty and is a former homeless youth.

Leigh is an inspiring and charismatic character with higher ambitions as a professional speaker, punk rocker, poet, and political pundit. He is covered in tattoos, bursting with opinions, and ready to set the world on fire.

https://www.facebook.com/leigh.z.bursey
https://www.linkedin.com/in/leighbursey
https://www.instagram.com/burseyleigh
https://www.twitter.com/leighbursey

Like you, Certified Money Coach® **Marlene Elizabeth** has heard the phrase "financial security" defined in numerous ways over the years. Is it a magic number you reach? Is it a lifestyle you live? Is it power and influence? Is it finally being debt-free? Is it meant for only a chosen few—those with a knack for numbers, a college degree, born from wealthy parents, or just plain "lucky"? Or is there a different story?

As a single mom and heart-centered leader who's risen from financial hardship to becoming a successful mamapreneur, Marlene's view is radically different. Her number-one international best-selling book, *Moneywings*™, is a spirit-filled love note full of inspiration for women to courageously embrace financial well-being.

Deeply motivated to be a financial role model for her daughter, Marlene coined the term *moneywings*™ to describe the feminine power of women to beautifully unfold their financial potential. Marlene believes when you realize your **freedom to soar,** you can't help but unfold your own beautiful moneywings™ one brave feather at a time.

Her deeply caring, strategic, spiritual, and innovative approach creates a safe-harbor for women to connect, learn, and grow. Through her online group and private one-on-one money coaching retreats, Marlene tenderly empowers women to create the income and impact they dream about.

Get started today with a *free money type quiz* at

www.UnfoldMoneyWings.com

Email: Marlene@MarleneElizabeth.com
Phone: 909.562.2159
Website: www.MeetWithMarlene.com
FB: www.facebook.com/growmoneywings
LinkedIn: www.linkedin.com/in/moneywings
Instagram: growmoneywings

Mary E. Knippel, Your Writing Mentor, is an international best-selling author, inspirational speaker, as well as the founder of Authentic Grace Communications. She is fiercely committed to helping high-achieving women to have compassion for their struggle in crafting the inspirational and transformational message they know they are tasked to deliver to the world. With a firm philosophy that "No one can tell your story except *you*," Mary invites you to take pen in hand to discern the wisdom of your life lessons with a keen awareness of the part synchronicity plays in all events, both big and small. Using her thirty-five years as a journalist and the power of storytelling, she is on a mission to support you to be visible, vibrant, and prosperous. Mary promises someone is indeed waiting to hear your story.

As a journal writer since the age of eleven, Mary views writing as a powerful companion, advisor, healing tool, and her number-one creative outlet. Marriage, raising a family, moving across the country (twice), and breast cancer (twice) all give her plenty of journal material to write about. Learn more about Mary's virtual classes and workshops, receive free writing tips and techniques, as well as what to do about writer's block, or invite her to speak to your group, by visiting her website at

https://yourwritingmentor.com.

Email: mary@yourwritingmentor.com
Phone: 650-440-5616
Website: https://yourwritingmentor.com
Facebook: https://fb.com/maryeknippel.author
Facebook: https://fb.com/maryeknippel
LinkedIn: https://www.linkedin.com/in/maryeknippel
Twitter: https://twitter.com/MEKnippelAuthor
YouTube: https://youtube.com/user/maryeknippel
Instagram: https://www.instagram.com/maryeknippelauthor

Maureen Ryan-Blake is the principal and founder of The Power of the Tribe.

The Power of the Tribe is a female solidarity group that serves women entrepreneurs to level-up their lives and business through the power of female friendship. Its mission is to help women find their focus and purpose and unlock their potential for greater success in business and life.

Maureen Ryan-Blake holds dual masters in leadership and diplomacy from SUNY Stony Brook. She is also a graduate of HCL Transformational Leadership and is committed to leading from generosity.

Maureen's professional career started on Wall Street, working with such companies as Cantor Fitzgerald and Newscorp. She moved on to develop a federal $6 million grant that connected hundreds of businesses and thousands of students, enabling the mentoring and coaching of youth and adults to find their purpose, unlock their potential, and step into a productive and engaging life. As a serial entrepreneur, Maureen has created several successful businesses and continues to align, serve, and support fellow entrepreneurs with genuine care and gratitude.

Maureen@thepoweofthetribe.com
https://thepoweofthetribe.com
619-852-4677 (private)
858-831-2220 (work)
https://www.facebook.com/thepoweofthetribenetwork
https://www.facebook.com/maureen.ryanblake
https://www.facebook.com/groups/thepoweofthetribe
linkedin.com/in/maureen-ryan-blake
https://twitter.com/MaureenRyanBla1
https://www.youtube.com/channel/UCmi6H1k635S5xfBHbkt2heA

Patrick P. Long is a father and widower born and raised in St. Louis, Missouri. While pursuing his lifelong ambition of being a writer, Patrick has earned his living as a systems engineer and database architect, which means he is a nerdy computer programmer.

Patrick has passions for aviation, sports, reading, writing, theater, music, movies, and popcorn. He eats way too much pizza and buffalo wings. He likes to binge-watch really good television shows.

Patrick has trained as a pilot and flown an airplane solo. He completed a grueling twenty-four-hour adventure race with four of his most insane friends. In training, Patrick flipped over the handlebars of his mountain bike and smashed face-first into a tree, somehow managing not to break his nose or knock out any teeth. What is even more embarrassing—and he doesn't want to admit—is that he did it again a week later.

Patrick's wife, Melanie, passed from breast cancer in 2019. Patrick is an active and avid supporter of the American Cancer Society and also Camp Kesem, a phenomenal camp and a child's friend through and beyond a parent's cancer.

Email: patrickp@patrickplong.com

Phone: 314-578-1897

Website: www.patrickplong.com

Facebook: facebook.com/patrickplong

LinkedIn: linkedin.com/in/patrick-p-long-author/

Twitter: @Paddymel

Rebecca Hall Gruyter is a global influencer, #1 international best-selling and award-winning author and compiler, in-demand publisher, empowering radio show host (reaching over 1 million listeners on eight networks), podcast host, and an empowerment leader that wants to help you reach more people. She has built multiple platforms to help experts reach more people. These platforms include: radio, TV, books, magazines, the Speaker Talent Search, and live events, creating a powerful promotional reach of over 10 million!

Rebecca is the CEO of RHG Media Productions (which includes the RHG TV network with over thirty weekly programs and a publishing arm that has helped 250+ authors become bestsellers). She is the owner of Your Purpose Driven Practice and the creator of the Speaker Talent Search.

RHG Media productions is an in-demand publisher that specializes in launching books as best sellers while creating great visibility both for the author and book. She helps the author be powerfully positioned and the star of their best-selling campaign to reach as many people as possible around the world.

Rebecca has personally contributed to over thirty published books, multiple magazines and has been quoted in Major Media, The Huffington Post, ABC, CBS, NBC, Fox, and Thrive Global. She has been recognized as one of the top ten working women in America by AWWIN, Inc., and now helps experts get quoted in major media too.

Today, she wants you to have impact! Be seen, heard, and SHINE!

Rebecca@YourPurposeDrivenPractice.com
www.facebook.com/rhallgruyter (Facebook)
www.YourPurposeDrivenPractice.com (Main Website)
www.RHGTVNetwork.com (TV network)
www.SpeakerTalentSearch.com (Free opportunity for speakers to get on more stages)
www.EmpoweringWomenTransformingLives.com (Weekly radio show)
www.AuthorsJourneyPodcast.com (Weekly podcast for authors)
www.MeetWithRebecca.com (Calendar link to schedule a time to talk with Rebecca)

Sarah Breen is a pediatrician practicing at Sanders Court Pediatrics in the northern suburbs of Chicago. She graduated from Washington University in St. Louis in 2004 with a degree in biology and a minor in psychology. She went on to medical school at Midwestern University and completed her pediatric residency at Lutheran General Hospital in Park Ridge, Illinois.

Sarah is married with two young sons and enjoys spending time with her family, exercise, and travel.

Sbbreen89@gmail.com

Shannon S. McKee is a communicator at heart. She is a writer, editor, and speaker. She writes at www. shannonsmckee.com. She coordinates the Women's Ministry at Redemption Chapel in Stow, Ohio, where she is a regular teacher, mentor, and Life Coach. She is passionate about helping women thrive from the inside out. She believes that leaving a legacy of excellence often comes in the quiet moments of the day-to-day as we open our lives and homes to others. Her other titles include grace-dweller, lover of Rick, momma to two, tea drinker, entrepreneur, putterer, and consumer of dark chocolate.

330-348-6410
communiqueVA@gmail.com
www.shannonsmckee.com
FB: https://www.facebook.com/ssmckee
FB: https://www.facebook.com/SSMcKeeBlog/
LinkedIn: https://www.linkedin.com/in/shannon-mckee-b657693a/
Instagram: https://www.instagram.com/ssmckee/

428 | BLOOM & SHINE!

Toni Stone Bruce knows what it means to have a dream and to have your life and dream shattered and broken. She knows what it means when God literally gives you a second chance, and you get to see that dream come to pass. From that, she has become an author, motivational speaker, and life coach. She is the CEO and founder of Precious Stones 4 Life, LLC, a training and development company that specializes in seminars, keynote speeches, and professional development workshops designed to enhance the physical, spiritual, emotional, and financial components of life. She teaches that life is worth living and that anyone can begin again, provided that they have precious stepping-stones, which she calls "gems," that point the way.

Preciousstones4life@gmail.com
321-350-7219
Facebook: Precious Stones 4 Life
Instagram: Precious Stones 4 Life

CLOSING THOUGHTS

We hope you have been touched by these powerful inspirations that have encouraged, equipped, and empowered you to *Bloom and Shine* each day of the year!

We hope you have been encouraged on your journey and are inspired to apply the practical and profound tips, advice, and great wisdom into your life. We can't wait to see you, hear from you, and celebrate you as you share the gift of you with the world! May you always choose to **Bloom & Shine no matter what may come. May you choose to step forward and shine one day and one inspiration at a time.**

Anthologies Available Now Compiled by Rebecca Hall Gruyter:

Special *Shine* Series
(Compiled and led by Rebecca Hall Gruyter)

Come out of Hiding and SHINE! (Book 1 in the *Shine* series)

Bloom Where You are Planted and Shine! (Book 2 in the *Shine* series)

Step Forward and Shine! (This book, the third and final book in the *Shine* series)

The Grandmother Legacies (Anthology compiled by Rebecca Hall Gruyter)

The Animal Legacies (Anthology compiled by Rebecca Hall Gruyter)

Empowering You, Transforming Lives (365-day inspiration compiled by Rebecca Hall Gruyter)

Special *Experts & Influencers* Series
(Compiled and led by Rebecca Hall Gruyter)

Experts & Influencers: The Leadership (Book 1 in the series)

Experts & Influencers: The Women's Empowerment (Book 2 in the series)

Experts & Influencers: Move Forward with Purpose! (Book 3; to be released in 2021)

Special Brilliance Series
(3-Book Series compiled and led by Rebecca Hall Gruyter)

Step Into Your Brilliance (Book 1 in the series)

Step Into Your Brilliant Mission & Purpose (Book 2; to be released in 2021

Journals Created by Rebecca Hall Gruyter:

The Animal Legacies Journal

Bloom & Shine Journal

Experts & Influencers: Leadership Journal

Experts & Influencers: Women's Empowerment Journal

Experts & Influencers: Move Forward with Purpose! (To be released in 2021)

Step Into Your Brilliance Journal

Step Into Your Brilliant Purpose Journal (To be released in 2021)

Books Available Now Featuring a Chapter or Section by Rebecca Hall Gruyter:

The 40/40 Rules Anthology compiled by Holly Porter

Becoming Outrageously Successful Anthology compiled by Dr. Anita Jackson

Bright Spots Compiled by Davis Creative

Catch Your Star Anthology published by THRIVE Publishing

Discover Your Destiny Anthology compiled by Denise Joy Thompson

Enlightened Women

Enlightened You Journal Compiled by Dr. Ruth Anderson

Gateway to an Enlightened World: Collective Life Lessons on Personal Transformation Anthology compiled by Dr. Ruth Anderson

I Am Beautiful Anthology compiled by Teresa Hawley-Howard

The Power of Our Voices, Sharing Our Story Anthology compiled by Teresa Hawley-Howard

Succeeding Against All Odds Anthology compiled by Sandra Yancey

Success Secrets for Today's Feminine Entrepreneurs Anthology compiled by Dr. Anita Jackson

Unstoppable Women of Purpose Anthology and workbook compiled by Nella Chikwe

Women on a Mission Anthology compiled by Teresa Hawley-Howard

Women of Courage, Women of Destiny Anthology compiled by Dr. Anita Jackson

Women Warriors Who Make It Rock Anthology compiled by Nichole Peters

You Are Whole, Perfect, and Complete - Just As You Are compiled by Carol Plummer and Susan Driscoll

Made in the USA
Las Vegas, NV
26 December 2020